Irina Belova-Smorzh

Being Healed
and Staying Alive

KYIV
2011

Belova-Smorzh I.
Being Healed and Staying Alive. – K., 2011. – 144 c.

Designed by Ananko Katya
Translated into English by Belenkaya Irina
Edited by Natalia Ioffe

The book of Irina Belova-Smorzh, who was healed from the third stage of cancer by the power of the Word of Living God, deals with a personal struggle with a terminal illness.

My heartfelt thanks to everyone who helped me make this book happen, especially to:
- The Holy Spirit for guiding me
- My mom and literary editor, Valeria Belova.
- My husband, Dmitry Smorzh
- Katya Ananko
- Irina Belenkaya
- Natalia Ioffe
- Nelya Lipatova
- Tatyana Zaichenko
- Irina Rozhkevich
- Tamara Nizhnik
- Veta Martzinovskaya
- Svetlana Bondarchuk
- Tatyana Bulatova
- Maria Kislyak
- Nina Hytraya
- Lyudmila Kovpak
- Lena Omelchenko

and many others who made this book possible

Contents

My Coming out from the Grave

(My testimony)

In 2005 I was diagnosed with cancer. I was also classified to be inoperable, because the cancer affected the bone. There was some time left to delay the impending death using traditional methods of therapy.

It happened right before my wedding. Our wedding guest list was was quickly replaced by long lists of doctors and prescriptions. After submitting a request to the local Marriage Hall, accompanied by my doctor's note we were quickly put ahead of the usual waiting list. We had no family members or friends with us on that day, (we had yet to prepare our parents for the serious changes in our lives). There was no wedding dress, no decorated limousines... We arrived to the marriage hall by public transportation, dressed casually in jeans , but with flowers

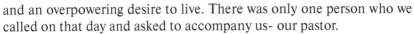

and an overpowering desire to live. There was only one person who we called on that day and asked to accompany us- our pastor.

The marriage hall's entire staff gathered to look at us, curious to see the young woman who wanted to be married before dying. We were pleasantly surprised that that they insisted on holding the full marriage ceremony for us, complete with the musical accompaniments and the great celebration hall, all free of charge!

And then I began the process of battling death and discovering the truth. I would not exchange that journey for the world. It is mine! And I walked it hand in hand with God! The Bible says: "You will know the truth and the truth shall set you free". You see, God Himself is the truth, and today I am free. It did not happen over a day, or a month, or a year. The way to learning the truth is long, narrow, and difficult, but also superior to anything else.

When I was checked into the hospital for treatment, I had two books with me: the Bible and F.F. Bosworth's book Christ the Healer. At that point the doctors were doing their job to help me and God in turn was doing His. I searched the Bible for scriptures about healing and marked them up with yellow post-its so that I could revisit them later on. I placed my hope into the Allmighty God. My Bible began to fill with little yellow bookmarks. I was looking for an answer, because the doctors had already given me theirs. When I was being checked into the hospital for treatment, undergoing preliminary tests and filling out paperwork, the doctor pulled my husband aside and advised him to begin planning his future. Her prognosis stated that he would soon become a widower. My parents were told the following by the medical staff, "This is pretty much a closed case. However, we will see what we can do."

I went through the entire grinder of the traditional medical treatments, and I allowed my body to be crushed to the point of no return. It so happened that, at the time, I did not know what I firmly believe today. I was not spiritually prepared for what was happening to me. Although I did have an understanding that God can heal, because once He had already stopped a deadly illness in my body. When it happened, my family and I received it as a miracle. Yet even that experience of God's mercy was not sufficient to resist cancer.

The doctors were under the impression that I did not fully understand the seriousness of my situation, because they always saw a smile on my face. I would walk around the hospital floors and pray for people. No one pushed me away. I tried to comfort people and told them the story of how God healed me once from an incurable illness. I would tell them that there is hope for them yet. People listened to me with genuine attention, but every now and again someone would ask, "Why then are you here now?" And then I did not know what to reply. The best I could come up with was, "I am here for you! To bring you hope and help you believe that God heals today."

I was walking along this path... Four cycles of exhausting treatments would be followed by a week of rest and reprieve, and then my body already half eaten by cancer would be once again boiled, poisoned by chemo, and killed over and over again with radiation...

I quickly began to lose weight. My legs hardly moved. I could not eat due to the acute intoxication of the organism...

Once, during an interval between treatments I was brought home. It was late autumn, and our house at the time was surrounded by a park. There were so many colors in the leaves of the trees! I asked to be helped to stand, with my feet buried in the multicolored carpet of the fallen leaves on the ground. I breathed them in, inhaling this autumn into my lungs, understanding that it could my last. Everything in me was being re-prioritised and re-evaluated. The only thing I remember not feeling was fear, as strange as it was... Ask any believer, whether they fear death? (I mean genuine believers, not just those who believe in the existence of God.) I think more often than not you will hear a negative response. In a strange and inexplicable way God gives us assurance in that which we cannot see. Thus with every cell of my body I felt then that He did not abandon me. I prayed, submerged myself in the Bible, prayed some more, then read about divine healing... In the short time that the doctors allowed me I would try to get to know God's will and His position regarding my situation. I felt the faith in the invisible and the impossible grow in me stronger than ever. Perhaps it sounds strange, but that time was a wondrous one. God was so close! And His strength was accomplished by my weakness.

In F.F. Bosworth's book, Christ the Healer, I read that we are the soil into which the seed of the Word of God is planted. I began to perceive the Bible differently. It is referred to as the word of life. I was thus sowing life into myself.

The last time I walked out of my doctor's office I was told, "There are no miracles." To which I answered, "You'd be surprised..." I was convinced that I would not return to that place under any circumstances. The reason for my discharge was that I could not withstand any more treatments. I was told to file for disability. Although I did not consider myself disabled, the doctors were not wrong in classifying me in this way. At the time of discharge my internal organs resembled a scrambled mess. I could practically feel my body coming apart at the seams, so to speak. There were parts of me with no skin covering the surface. All the functions of the organism responsible for resisting death were completely disabled. I had no physical strength left. I understood that no one and nothing could help me at that point, except God.

Returning home meant entering another battlefield. The subsequent effects of radiation treatments are unpredictable and can manifest themselves in the most horrific ways. I lost the skin of my entire mouth cavity, and it felt like being flayed alive. There were puss filled sores and unspeakable pain... I was unable to sleep or eat, and could hardly drink anything. Each turn of the head would cause a blood flow and a bout of pain so strong it would send my body into violent tremors... Pain medication brought no relief.

I spent over seven days in this state. I prayed ceaselessly. I was desperate for God's intervention! When my husband left for church to attend all-night prayer, the entire congregation prayed for me. That night I finally slept, and in my sleep I could feel that the illness had loosened its grip on me. In the morning I could feel my wounds begin to heal. God never left me. He was leading me out of death.

My home computer was set up so that I could watch television programs on it. Monday through Friday at 7:30 am, the NTN channel would broadcast "Believer's Voice of Victory" with Kenneth and Gloria Copeland. A sermon for each day, and often a message of healing. My husband would record the program in the morning and throughout the day I would listen to it over and over again. I would go over the scriptures mentioned in the program, immerse myself in God's presence, contemplate, repeat and review... Believe.

And then the day came, when I was able to throw a bagful of prescription drugs into the garbage can. Although I still had pain, I saw no point in taking the drugs anymore. Something changed in me! My faith in God rose above everything that I could physically see and feel.

Slowly and gradually, I began to get back on my feet, go back to work, pick up the blueprints again...

...Today I hardly remember the way to the hospital. I do not depend on doctors and do not take medications. All my internal organs are functioning well. I am healthy and happy. I am a person who believes in the Mighty God, and in miracles. I have been taught by the Lord how to resist the disease and pain of this world. The laws of this world lead to destruction and death, and people perish along with it. However, there are laws which are not of this world, that allow us to live according to a different nature: without sickness and disease, without defeat or need. For this to become a reality we must learn from the One Who set those laws in motion. He is the Doctor, able and willing to cure all sickness, soothe all the pain, ready to create new kidneys, eyes, teeth... He is the Creator.

Believe me, I know what I am talking about. I am begging you to believe!

With a prayer for your healing
having twice risen from the grave
Irina Belova-Smorzh

Why did this book need to be born?

Foreword

Proverbs 24:11
Deliver those who are drawn toward death, And hold back those stumbling to the slaughter.

John 3:16
For God so loved the world that He gave His only begotten Son, that whoever believes in Him should not perish but have everlasting life.

1Peter 2:24
...who Himself bore our sins in His own body on the tree, that we, having died to sins, might live for righteousness — by whose stripes you were healed.

This book is for those people who know what it's like to be sent home to die with the words, «We've done everything we could...».

This book is for all those who feel helpless, whose efforts to restore to life their terminally ill loved ones have failed.

This book is for those who are exhausted by endless medications and hospital visits.

This book is for those who have been attending church for many years, but continue to struggle with disease in their bodies, frequently visit the doctor, spend a great deal of money on surgeries and do not have a revelation that it is not the way it should be.

This book is also for those who do not attend church, but wish to be healthy and whole, even if it means turning to God for help...

This book is for those who wish to learn how to live healthy and stay healthy: without sickness and pain, without worrying about what the next winter's flu may bring, without helplessness and despair that everything has been tried, and nobody on the earth can stop cancer, HIV, asthma, schizophrenia... and help others...

In this book I will speak about the Only One Who is powerful to heal today. I find it difficult to be silent, having experienced the power of the resurrection in action in my own life. I do not want people to have to die when there is a real way out of any terminal illness. It is not a myth, it is the truth about God's grace. I share this message everywhere: in the newspapers, on the radio, during church services. I teach what I have learned, and am still learning.

I present to you a handbook on how to battle diseases.

I gathered everything I have said, written and preached on the radio for those who are suffering from an illness and for those who seek for help for their loved ones.

I am adding my testimony about my experience of coming out from the grave as well as some testimonies of people whose lives I have been a witness to and a part of, but mostly Biblical stories and verses of the Scripture. I also used testimonies and experience of renowned God's generals: John G. Lake, Smith Wigglesworth, Kenneth E. Hagen, Oral Roberts, Katherine Kulman... and also God's teachers and witnesses of God's healing power of nowadays: Kenneth and Gloria Copeland, Makhesh Chavda and Benny Hinn... Their great work and feat of faith influenced my resurrection.

I would not be able to learn so much about Jesus as the Healer on my own in such a short period of time as I did. I did not have enough time to become a giant of faith. When the process of dying has begun in my body, I had to put a stop to it with the process of faith. I had been going to church for a long time. I had seen a lot of healing miracles done by the Holy Spirit, but there had been no SCHOOL of healing at the time. We were not taught to lean on God's truth for support in order to be able to "take a punch" and then fight off all weakness and disease. Today I keep learning this and I thank God for people who helped my quest for knowledge about His healing truth!

This is, in fact, a guide for fighting against disease, a technique I used to escape the clutches of death with a claim to divine health. I preach to you the true healing of Jesus Christ, as all of these principles I list come directly from the Word of God – the Bible. Believe me, that all other methods in attempt to survive a terminal illness inevitably lead to disappointment. They result in a waste of time, money and strength. It is the kind of life that quickly exhausts all involved: you and the family members who look after you.

God wants us to seek Him as the Healer. He is prepared to give us the answers to all of our problems. He desires to heal His children! He loves us so much! He tore the curtain in the temple that separated Him from man. Today everything is accessible to us. However, if we do not know any of this, then we cannot accept what He has prepared for us. Having learned the truth we need to receive it from His hands, from His words, from the Bible.

These things which I write are not based on my personal opinion. The only real compass of truth is the Word of God. I am certain that, if you seek, you will find there are people around you who know more than you about it, and who can teach you. They can help you, and make the process of learning about your Creator and Healer clear and simple. None of us have descended from apes. The One Who created us made no mistake. He had not created us for suffering, disease and curses. He created us very well indeed. If we are broken, He stands ready to fix us up. He is our Father. He does not want us to be destroyed by disease. He loves to make us happy.

I can help you today by sharing with you everything that I know about it. Like never before I believe that, when the Gospel is preached, the word being spoken attracts God's healing power like a magnet. The sound of the word about divine healing attracts miracles. God never changes. He heals today just as He healed 2000 years ago. As He raised men from the dead, He does it today. He delivers. He comforts. He saves. He protects... He does it, because of His great mercy, but according to our faith. As a Doctor He does His job very well. Our part is to trust Him.

You can let God come into your life even now, and He will heal you. Or you can put this book aside. But if you dare to believe God about your healing, you will be set free from any weakness, pain, disease and death. In order to trust the God Whom you do not see more than your own symptoms, which you feel, you need to get to know Him as a Healer, to get know Him intimately. It will not be easy. Perhaps it will not be quick. You will need to work hard, but your life is truly worth it.

One athlete, with whom my husband competed in the veterans swimming championship in Sweden, had a slogan printed on his T-shirt: "The pain of self-discipline is easier to take than the pain of disappointment".

If you discipline yourself in order to train your spirit according to the Word of God and you remain faithful in it, no disease can stay in your body. It will retreat, if you resist it. The point is to understand: like any other miracles, healing comes only from God.

Begin by praying to Him.

Heavenly Father! Forgive me all my sins! Forgive me for living without You for such a long time! Come into my life, Jesus! I confess You as my Lord and Saviour! Be my Healer! I need You! I believe that You died for me on the Cross and rose again on the third day. I believe that Your Blood washed away all of my sins and diseases, and by Your stripes I am healed. I give You my life. I give into Your loving hands my spirit, soul and body. I thank You for accepting me the way I am, forgiving me and healing my soul and body. Right now by faith I receive life without disease and pain. Thank You, Father!

If you do not have the Bible, get one. Let it be in your native language or any other that you can easily read and clearly understand. You need to plunge headfirst into the Bible. It is the word that will heal you. When you see in my book the Scripture verses, open your Bible, look for these words, abide in them... It is a miraculous process. I will help you. Prepare to be healed and be healthy! In the name of Jesus!

Chapter 1

J am the Lord your healer

**_Exodus 15:25,26_
25. So he cried out to the LORD, and the LORD showed him a tree. When he cast it into the waters, the waters were made sweet. There He made a statute and an ordinance for them, and there He tested them,
26. and said, "If you diligently heed the voice of the LORD your God and do what is right in His sight, give ear to His commandments and keep all His statutes, I will put none of the diseases on you which I have brought on the Egyptians. For I am the LORD who heals you."

God offers us to accept Him as the Healer. The only Healer, so that there would be nothing broken and nothing missing within us. He always gives us a choice.

**_Deuteronomy 30:15_
"See, I have set before you today life and good, death and evil...

**_Deuteronomy 30:19_
I call heaven and earth as witnesses today against you, that I have

set before you life and death, blessing and cursing; therefore choose life, that both you and your descendants may live.

It is always up to us: to choose His way of healing or our own way (the one we're used to, one the whole world follows, a tangible way, which can be analyzed...).

We often choose an easier way — we limit ourselves to taking medicine, which only reduces pain or visual symptoms of disease. However, medicine does not remove the source of illness, because the root of illness lies in the invisible spiritual dimension. Medicine cannot penetrate into this dimension. It is a spiritual issue, and it should be solved on a spiritual level.

> *From the book of Kenneth E. Hagin* "*The basics of spiritual growing*» *(Lesson 9* "*Faith and senses*", *page 22)*
> *God's healing is a spiritual healing. If medicine heals, it heals physically. "Christian science" heals through mind, but when God heals, He heals through spirit.*

Do not limit yourself by relying on doctors alone. God desires to give you much more — His healing. In reality He has already done it. Our part is to receive it, while trusting Him.

It is not enough to ease the pain and be satisfied. The pain has feet. It is obliged to leave the person who has been redeemed. The pain must be forbidden, by the power of Jesus Who has won over it. Otherwise the pain will wait until the painkiller wears off and then come back to spread itself all over the body as a consequence of the disease, the root of which remains. It is such a pity that we can consent to surgical operation, but at the same time refuse the hand of the Almighty Healer. It is not enough to get rid of the pain if the tumour is still there. When the pain abates, we get a temporary respite and feel a sense of relief. That is why we do not have a desire to spend time seeking God's face. We have a lot of things to do, which draw us away from God. This is nothing new under the sky. We can see in the Bible, book of Exodus, that the Pharaoh had the same mentality as we have today.

**_Exodus, 8:15_
But when Pharaoh saw that there was relief, he hardened his heart and did not heed them, as the LORD had said.

While the Pharaoh suffered the stinging of flies, the plague of frogs, he called out to the God of Moses for help and was prepared to accept all of His conditions. However, when some relief came, Pharaoh returned to his old self: with his old stronghold, anger and envy... In fact, these emotions, if given free reign, cause diseases in us today. They destroy our souls and then ruin our flesh.

God gives us His ways of healing. Jesus and the word of God open these ways for us.

The Bible is called the Book of Life, the living Word. The word of God is living and active.

**_Hebrew 4:12_
For the word of God is living and powerful, and sharper than any two-edged sword, piercing even to the division of soul and spirit, and of joints and marrow, and is a discerner of the thoughts and intents of the heart.

It always fulfills its purpose.

**_Isaiah 55:11_
So shall My word be that goes forth from My mouth; It shall not return to Me void, But it shall accomplish what I please, And it shall prosper in the thing for which I sent it.

God has already sent His healing word to Earth in the person of Jesus Christ, therefore we have everything to keep us from perishing.

**_Psalm 107:20_
He sent His word and healed them, And delivered them from their destructions.

He sent His word over 2000 years ago. Today every man can either accept this fact or not. Why did God do this?

**_John 3:15,16_
15. that whoever believes in Him should not perish but have eternal life.
16. For God so loved the world that He gave His only begotten Son, that whoever believes in Him should not perish but have everlasting life.

Should not perish! Should not perish! Do you wish not to perish in this dying world? Do you want to be completely healthy in this sickly world? Do you want to be safe among the world's many dangers?.. Let us continue to look into this question.

What happened on the cross of Calvary 2000 years ago?

**_Isaiah 53:4-6_
4. Surely He has borne our grieves And carried our sorrows; Yet we esteemed Him stricken, Smitten by God, and afflicted.
5. But He was wounded for our transgressions, He was bruised for our iniquities; The chastisement for our peace was upon Him, And by His stripes we are healed.
6. All we like sheep have gone astray; We have turned, every one, to his own way; And the LORD has laid on Him the iniquity of us all.

He took upon Himself all of our sins, which were the primary causes of our diseases. Where there is a sin, there are sure to be diseases. If there is no sin, there is nothing for diseases to take hold of. Jesus achieved victory by His own death and destroyed the power of sin, infirmity, diseases and death.

**_1Peter 2:24_
Who Himself bore our sins in His own body on the tree, that we, having died to sins, might live for righteousness — by whose stripes you were healed.

We have been healed. We have been redeemed. We have been paid for by the blood of Jesus. The soul is in the blood. A sacrifice has been made for every single soul. We will never be able to repay God's sacrifice for it was priceless. He did it unconditionally, with His great love and according to Christ's grace. Because of the great grace of God you and I did not perish. It is not because you have a good personality, not because you have never done anyone harm, not because you love animals and care for them, not because there are good doctors among your friends... but according to God's grace.

>   *From the book of John G. Lake "The power above demons, diseases and death" (page 105, chapter 11 "The grace of God's healing")*
>
>   *I want to use the text which is familiar to you:"For the grace of God that brings salvation has appeared to all men" (Titus 2:11). There has never been anything greater than the word "GRACE". If we analyze all the effects of grace, this beautiful word will clearly reveal the versatility of the Gospel of Jesus Christ. The grace of Jesus Christ is not His favor nor His generous donation. It is a supernatural outpouring of God's nature, heavenly healing love and holy balsam. It comes to the world in need not only as an action by God, which saves from the sin, but also as a healing grace which goes through a human nature and reduces pain; changes chemical processes in body so that it becomes healthy; blesses a man with salvation, healing and eternal comfort in God. God's healing is not a mystery, but quite definite action of God's Spirit in human souls and bodies.*

All healing miracles happen on the earth by the power of the Holy Spirit. He is omnipresent. He is everywhere. That is why your Doctor is near you now. If you are reading this book, you have already opened the door to Him.

Oh! This is a wonderful way. Believe me, when you are recovering hand-in-hand with Him, your healing will no longer be your aim. The true treasure of the rest of your new life will be a close relationship with your Healer and Maker.

He makes everything new. If you need new organs, He will make them for you. You will ask me where my new organs came from. God has renewed me. How could it happen? I do not know. I am not trying to sort it out, but I know for certain that my body was practically eaten by cancer and finished off by conventional medicine, but now I am living a complete and enjoyable life without doctors and medicines. After a series of complex procedures in the Cancer Center my organs were a solid burned mush, they were literally stuck together!.. I was more dead than alive. I remember leaving my body at times... Doctors are merely human beings. There is a lot that they do not know, they sometimes experiment and take chances, sometimes make mistakes... They do this just as other professionals do: engineers, architects, builders for example. Sometimes the building goes to ruin because of the extreme pressures that were not accounted for.

God does not make mistakes. He knows everything and can do everything, thus He does not experiment. He is the Author. We are His creation. If our body has gone out of order, He alone knows how to mend us. Do you agree with me?

A man is not a sovereign creature. He was made according to certain laws that keep him intact. If we break these laws, destruction takes its course. That is why a man cannot live without his Maker. He has to be in unity with the source of his life. Otherwise he is dead to the peace in his heart, to the happiness of his family, to his children being blessed and not prone to addictions; to the love which is not self-seeking; to joy and laughter without the aid of alcohol; to the true prosperity without dependence on money; to boundless health and a deep-rooted faith.

**1John 5:11,12
11. And this is the testimony: that God has given us eternal life, and this life is in His Son.
12. He who has the Son has life; he who does not have the Son of God does not have life.

I am an architect. I am the author of many beautiful projects. It is the story of my creative life. I can change any of my projects and create something better. I am an author. God is the Author above all authors. Nothing is impossible for Him. He is the One Who has the right and ability to create and improve our souls and our bodies.

> *From the book of Kathryn Kuhlman* "I believe in miracles"
> ...The doctor who is coming to the sick man's room is not alone. He can help someone who is in need by instruments of scientific medicine, but his faith in the highest power does the rest.
> ..."All healings have divine nature", Doctor Elmer Gess says.
> A doctor can join broken bones, but they will knit under the influence of divine power. A surgeon can successfully provide a difficult surgery, he can be a true master of the scalpel and he can use the foremost knowledge, but he must expect that the highest power will complete the real healing. People are not given the ability of healing.

There is a firm opinion in the minds of many that God's healing is outdated, that it was characteristic to the early Church only. Other people think that God heals only select individuals, and you never know whether He will heal you or not. However, we are the same Church! The Church is not is not defined by walls. It is all the people who belong to Jesus Christ. We are born again in the same Spirit! We all have the same promises. God has always guaranteed the healing to His people. Remember, He is the only One Who heals today.

It is careless to think that it will all come out all right in the end, and the tumour will dissipate by itself:"How can it be? I have repented!" You must not forget that the world we live in is under the control of the evil one.

One woman, a year-and-a-half after being diagnosed with cancer was thinking carelessly: "I thought that it would go away somehow ..." It will never happen unless someone assumes the authority and puts everything in its right place by the word of faith and by the power of the Holy Spirit. In order to use the authority and power of Spirit we need to use our faith, know the word of God and His will. This is the way. It takes time. After you become strengthened by God and His power, go on and move "the mountains", "the mountains" of weakness and disease. For everything is possible for him who believes, who believes that Jesus is almighty. And we are in Him. We can do nothing without Him. That is why we must abide in Him and in His word. He has left us specific instructions on how to live a victorious life and not have to die in our prime, or because of the calamities of this world. He separated us from this world. We cannot see with our physical eyes His covering hand which separates, protects and leads us, but we feel it in our heart. That is why we rest and dwell in the shelter of the Most High. Every family, every house lives in this shelter. Every breath is under His cover. If we want our family, our house, and our every breath to be under His protection, we need to believe in it.

I want to include in my book a passage from the book of Makhesh Chavda. I want to quote it practically whole, because such life stories of the people of faith are testimonies for us who follow in their footsteps, revelations of God's mercy and love of and the closeness of His healing presence. I often re-read this chapter and it inspires me. All of us need to become confident in the help of God. We all need it!

<u>*From the book of Mahesh Chavda*</u> *"Hidden power of touching of the believer"(chapter 1 "The Lord is our Healer")*
...A few days ago my wife Bonny delivered Benjamin, our first-born... Standard examination revealed a serious problem. "At first I thought it was a malignant tumour", said the doctor, "but it turned out worse, much worse. Your son has a congenital kidney disease. The main part of kidneys was already affected in the womb"... We were told that Benjamin would die in a few weeks or in better case in a few months, because the infection will kill the rest of kidney tissue.

We were not ready for such outcome, we did not want it. For a few days and weeks, while Benjamin was faintly clinging to life, the Holy Spirit had been testing my walking in faith. I fasted and prayed for my son. I tried to find all verses about healing in the Scripture, wrote them out, put the name of my son in the text. Then I proclaimed that healing especially for him:"By His stripes my son Benjamin is healed. God sends His Word and heals my son Benjamin". I did it day by day writing out and proclaiming the Scripture, meditating and praying.

The doctors did their best and advised us:"Pray, because we cannot give Benjamin new kidneys".

After surgery Benjamin had drains and tubes that went from his urinary bladder and his kidneys. He screamed with pain. The nurses cried and said:"It is a pity we cannot give him a painkiller, because it will stop his heart".

Benjamin was put in a special ward where he was connected to the electronic equipment which controlled his vital rates. We were told that he would constantly suffer pain. Benjamin cried all the time, the signal on the monitor went up and down, reacting on the traumas in his tiny body and showed the intensity of sensation of pain...

We wanted desperately to hold him in our hands, to hug him, kiss him, to drive away the terrible pain by our love, but our son was slowly dying in torments, and we were so helpless.

I remember I went out and prayed:"Lord, I shared Your word all around the world, I saw endless quantity of people, who came to Christ; I witnessed about signs and miracles of healing to thousands of people. Now I need to experience it personally. My family and I need to know that Jesus has taken our weaknesses and diseases and "by His stripes we have been healed".

When a few hours later we were let in the special ward, where Benjamin was, the nurse, who still had tears in her eyes, said:"Something is going on".

My heart sank:"Is he dying?"

"No, sir. Look at the monitor".

The signal on the monitor went up and down like it had gone before. I said:"He is still suffering strong pain".

The nurse replied:"No, sir. I do not understand, but look at your son".

I walked away from the monitor and looked at precious little Benjamin. He was soundly sleeping stretching his arms and smiling. He was surrounded by bright golden light and was blissfully calm. According to the readings on monitor he was suffering unbearable pain. The doctors compared such pain with the pain which women usually experience during delivery. But it was obvious that Benjamin did not feel anything like that. That evening, at that time, I did not know how I realized that Jesus took his pain. Like never before I knew the truth that "by His stripes we are healed". In some mysterious way Benjamin

was connected to the power of God to the event which happened two thousand years ago on Golgotha. God was healing my son!
   A few days ago an x-ray showed that the kidneys of Benjamin were viable and completely restored! The doctors could not explain that. They assumed that previous x-ray analysis was wrong, but I knew what had happened! Jesus took the pain of my son and literally raised his kidneys from the dead!

You have yet to walk this path, experience the process of getting to know the healing Word. There is nothing hidden in your experiences with God, that will not be revealed. If you received a revelation from Him, it will become flesh within you. Your body will receive it.

Prepare the way for the Lord from within yourself, from within your soul. We need to renew our mind concerning the knowledge that God is the Healer. He is the only One Who heals today. By His stripes we are healed. It will not be taken from us.

"For I am the LORD who heals you."(Exodus 15:26)

Please pray with me.
   Heavenly Father! Let me get to know You as my personal Healer! I want to fully receive Your word that by Your stripes my family and I were healed. Jesus! Help me comprehend Your truth which freed me from sickness, disease, any affliction and addiction of this world. I choose Your ways. I set my hopes upon You alone. You know all of my problems and needs. I cannot solve them without You. I believe that You love me and care for me as a loving Father and Lord Almighty. I know and believe that my Healer is near. You are the Lord who heals me!

Chapter 2

Now acquaint yourself with Him, and be at peace

**_Job 22:21-30_

21. "Now acquaint yourself with Him, and be at peace; thereby good will come to you.

22. Receive, please, instruction from His mouth, and lay up His words in your heart.

23. If you return to the Almighty, you will be built up; you will remove iniquity far from your tents.

24. Then you will lay your gold in the dust, and the gold of Ophir among the stones of the brooks.

25. Yes, the Almighty will be your gold and your precious silver;

26. For then you will have your delight in the Almighty, and lift up your face to God.

27. You will make your prayer to Him, He will hear you, and you will pay your vows.

28. You will also declare a thing, and it will be established for you; so light will shine on your ways.

29. When they cast you down, and you say, 'Exaltation will come!'
then He will save the humble person.
30. He will even deliver one who is not innocent; yes, he will be deliv-
ered by the purity of your hands."

**Hebrews 11:6
But without faith it is impossible to please Him, for he who comes to
God must believe that He is, and that He is a rewarder of those who
diligently seek Him.

For He is... He is... What is He like? Where is He? Where am I to seek Him? Where am I to go? What is the address? How am I to speak to Him?...

Everything is very simple. The relationship with God is really quite simple. We often tend to make everything more complicated than it should be.

He exists! And He is Love.

**1John 4:15,16
Whoever confesses that Jesus is the Son of God, God abides in him,
and he in God. And we have known and believed the love that God
has for us. God is love, and he who abides in love abides in God, and
God in him.

In fact, all the commandments, which God has given us, come down to that of love: love... When we follow these commandements – all is well.

**Mathew 22:36-40
36. "Teacher, which is the great commandment in the law?"
37. Jesus said to him, " 'You shall love the LORD your God with all
your heart, with all your soul, and with all your mind.'
38. This is the first and great commandment.
39. And the second is like it: 'You shall love your neighbor as yourself.'
40. On these two commandments hang all the Law and the Prophets."

God created everything according to His laws of love. He Himself is that love. For as long as man depended on Him, He ruled his life, and everything was good. When a man lost touch with the source of life, everything was ruined. It is impossible to walk in love without a source of love. God desires to once again give everyone a life filled with love, because everything is created according to the genetics of His love. His love is defined by the word "agape". "Agape" is always unconditional love. It means:"I will love you in spite of everything". This love never fails.

> ****_1Cor. 13:4-8_**
> *4. Love suffers long and is kind; love does not envy; love does not parade itself, is not puffed up;*
> *5. does not behave rudely, does not seek its own, is not provoked, thinks no evil;*
> *6. does not rejoice in iniquity, but rejoices in the truth;*
> *7. bears all things, believes all things, hopes all things, endures all things.*
> *8. Love never fails.*

Love never fails. When my husband and I were told by the doctors that the diagnosis was "cancer", it was like a death sentence, the ultimate defeat. We had just found each other. We had been preparing for our wedding, not for loss. We did not want to acknowledge defeat. We began seeking God, and He showed my husband this Scripture: Love never fails. This word had been keeping us strong for a long time... It is still keeps us strong today.

The Lord is very close to you. He is nearer than your own breath. Where is your heart today? Is it close enough to Him that He could change you and raise you up for a new life?

The illustration:

What happens to a litmus paper when it is dipped into the special solution? It changes its appearance. Being saturated with this solution it takes on the characteristics that are known to its creator. The creator alone knows what way it is supposed to be. From the very beginning it has all necessary components to be transformed. What does it need? It needs to be completely immersed into a new environment, does it not? It needs to be saturated with this environment, and then the transformation will happen. In Jesus Christ we are being transformed into His likeness. Being immersed into His presence, being saturated with the Holy Spirit, being strengthened by His power we reflect the intentions of the Heavenly Father. His will is our divine health. God wants to see all of us healthy. He loves us. He is the Father.

Accept Him as your loving Father, as your Friend, as your Defender, as your Only Almighty Doctor. Just come to Him. He desires to heal and comfort us, to take away our pain and to fortify us in the face of the suffering in this world.

> ****_Mathew 11:28_**
> **Come to Me, all you who labor and are heavy laden, and I will give you rest.**

Are you wondering where you would need to go? Well, where would you like to meet Jesus? Wherever you are, whatever your surroundings, just close your eyes, abstract yourself for a moment from all the problems and hassles and imagine yourself before Jesus. God is everywhere. It is not difficult for Him to come to you. He is omnipresent. He wants to be near you. He always waits for this moment. He asks that we find time for Him. That is why He established the seventh day of the week as a day when, instead of occupying ourselves with our daily routines, we should spend it with Him, reading His word and praying. When we are close to Him – all is well with us. He is always with us. His promise is always in effect:

> ****_Hebrews 13:5_**
> **...For He Himself has said, "I will never leave you nor forsake you"...**

> ****_Mathew 28:20_**
> **I am with you always, even to the end of the age.**

We need to take the first step towards Him, then the second... and keep going. Towards Him...

> ****_James 4:8_**
> **Draw near to God and He will draw near to you.**

Jeremiah 33:3
Call to Me, and I will answer you, and show you great and mighty things, which you do not know.

Is there a thing today that falls beyond your understanding? Cancer being healed? Being raised from the dead? Complete rejuvenation at the age of 80? Functioning new organs in the body, which were amputated by the surgeon 5 years ago?...God promises: "I will show you great and mighty things! I will!"

When we are born again, when we become Christians, we also receive God's own nature. From that moment on — we belong to Him.

Isaiah 43:1-4
1. But now, thus says the LORD, who created you, O Jacob, and He who formed you, O Israel: " Fear not, for I have redeemed you; I have called you by your name; you are Mine.
2. When you pass through the waters, I will be with you; and through the rivers, they shall not overflow you. When you walk through the fire, you shall not be burned, nor shall the flame scorch you.
3. For I am the LORD your God, the Holy One of Israel, your Savior; I gave Egypt for your ransom, Ethiopia and Seba in your place.
4. Since you were precious in My sight, you have been honored, and I have loved you; therefore I will give men for you, and people for your life.

He paid a high price in order to gain us in Jesus Christ. We became co-heirs with Jesus. We were healed by His wounds, received an abundance of blessing through Jesus, found salvation and eternal life. The righteous has the same heritage for his descendants.

Proverbs 11:21
Though they join forces, the wicked will not go unpunished; but the posterity of the righteous will be delivered.

He knows all our needs before we ask. There is no need that He can deny. There is no disease that He did not lay down at the cross of Calvary.

Only His Spirit can help us understand the full extent of all this. Today we are surrounded by His Spirit. He breathes next to us. How do I know this to be true? Because the Holy Spirit is present every time Jesus is spoken about. The Holy Spirit is present where the Gospel is being preached. Today He is among us. Distance is no obstacle for Him. He is everywhere. He is everything. Everything happens through Him. Our healing is accomplished by Him and through Him. Let Him envelope you within Himself, dissolve Himself into you, let Him look into your eyes...

And then everything invisible to the human eye will become real in the presence of God's Spirit. I will feel Him with all my heart, my own spirit. To believe with my heart means to know in my spirit. I am a spirit, not a body. Whatever your body is telling you now: "I feel pain...", "it is incurable...", "I am so weak...", just let your spirit burst out and connect with the Holy Spirit of God.

The body will always contradict the spirit. It will argue, complain and resist. That is why we must get stronger in the spirit so that we could rule over any disorders in our body.

We will never manage to solve our problems on earth without God's help. We must constantly ask our Father for help. He loves responding to us, when we appeal to Him. Appealing to Him is what our prayer is. God loves making us happy, revealing Himself to us in all His magnificence... He is ready to share His secrets with us!.. He is a God of miracles!.. As long as we believe!

He gives us a guarantee that He will always answer our prayers. He speaks volumes about this!

For every answer we seek, we need to look in the Word of God. We should put the Bible before our eyes and "taste that the Lord is good."

**_Joshua 1:8_
This Book of the Law shall not depart from your mouth, but you shall meditate in it day and night, that you may observe to do according to all that is written in it. For then you will make your way prosperous, and then you will have good success.

Our problem is that our mindset has not been renewed. God wants to give us His own. He wants us to behave wisely according to His perspective, and only then everything will work out. If we adopt God's mindset we will no longer live in fear of the next disease. We will not be threatened by financial problems, when everybody talks about a world crisis. We will see everything with His eyes. We will think in accordance with His Word. We will do what He does. We will always be healthy, prosperous and successful in every good work; our children will be taught by God; we will live life to the fullest: we will be strong and cheerful; we will live by faith, not by sight, because we will know Him.

Study the Scriptures. Meditate on the words of the Bible day and night, so that you may know what is good according to God's view and what is not. Learn to behave in the way God teaches us.

**John 8:32
And you shall know the truth, and the truth shall make you free.

As we get to know the truth, our souls and our bodies will be healed miraculously. We will become different. We will become the way He knows us to be and we will know Him intimately.

**1 Corinthians 13:12
For now we see in a mirror, dimly, but then face to face. Now I know in part, but then I shall know just as I also am known.

We will know Him as a Healer. We should strive to rid ourselves of diseases, not put up with them. We should give our body to God. How? Spend every day in His presence, in His word. Offer Him the sacrifice of time. Do not waste your time seeking the best doctors. Sooner or later you will hear: "We have done our best".

Spend your time in His Word that heals. This is the way that leads to divine health, to life without countless medications, without end-less doctor's appointments, without exhausting procedures and treatment expenses. Do you want to have divine health? Dare to take a step much farther than your local hospital, into the territory of God's presence.

**_Job 22:21_
Now acquaint yourself with Him, and be at peace; thereby good will come to you.

Draw near to God so that you can be saturated with Him to the bottom of your heart, and then have a great abundance of Him, so that He may shine from within you. Prepare a straight way for Him. Let Him humble you. You will be well. God did not create a man to be tortured by painful illnesses. He created a perfect man in His own image. When His work was done He saw that it was very good. If your life does not look very good today, let God improve everything. Let Him teach you to be happy. He wants it much more than you. For it is for His glory, when those who are oppressed by illnesses become set free, when an incurable disease surrenders, when the dead comes back to life...

What does it take from us? It takes time, effort, humbleness and trust. In order for God to deliver us from an incurable disease it is not enough to read the Bible for 20 minutes and shed tears before a religious icon for 10 minutes. The way to get healed is to draw nearer to God. This is the way according to His laws, which He gave us, so that we would not perish but have a full and happy life. There is no life without Him. We seem to be alive when in the morning we open our eyes. We are dead unless God is in our spirit. There is a law of the Spirit of life, which saves us. This law is in Jesus Christ: "...because through Christ Jesus the law of the Spirit of life set me free from the law of sin and death."(Romans 8:2)

Jesus is the Word of God. Those who are in Him will be preserved in life. If we refuse submitting to the laws of life, it is natural that we are eventually destroyed. We should learn to live according to the supernatural laws of God, learn to live by faith, not by sight. We should refrain from speaking if there is any doubt or disbelief in our mind. We should learn not to be affected by people's reactions; call things that are not as though they are; repent for our mistakes on the spot; and ALWAYS, ALWAYS, ALWAYS remain in HIM, in His Word, in Jesus. He is our desease-free and weakness-free life, life without debts and loans, without fear and defeat. God is ready to reveal His affluence to us. Who is prepared to accept it today? We should always expect it, in spite of the things we see, putting the past behind us and strive ahead, into His healing presence...

Say this prayer with me
Heavenly Father! Thank You for Your everlasting love to me!

Thank You that I can always be in Your presence through the blood of the Lord Jesus Christ. My God! How endless is Your love to me. You have given Your Son ...... for me and my children! You saved me. You took me out of disease and death. You healed my life. Let me know it with all my nature! I call upon You so that You show me all great and unknown things I do not know.

Draw me close to You, to Your healing presence. I want to bow before You with honor. I believe that You are near, by Your Spirit. You will not leave me nor forsake me. You will never turn away from me nor push me away ... I can close my eyes and put down my head on Your lap... I can touch Your hands by my spirit... I can hide in You... You are as close as Your peace that covers me, comforts my heart and heals my wounds.

Find a rest in God only, my soul!

Chapter 3

Without Him nothing was made

**John 1:1,3*
1. In the beginning was the Word, and the Word was with God, and the Word was God.
3. All things were made through Him, and without Him nothing was made that was made.

Every beginning is from Him, from His Word. No healing begins without Him. Look at these words carefully: without Him nothing was made. If we need healing to begin, we need the Word of healing, and then the healing will come. Healing is not just a process. It is a person — Jesus Christ. You wonder how it can be? The answer is in the Scripture.

**John 1:14,15*
14. And the Word became flesh and dwelt among us, and we beheld His glory, the glory as of the only begotten of the Father, full of grace and truth.

15. John bore witness of Him and cried out, saying, "This was He of whom I said, 'He who comes after me is preferred before me, for He was before me.'"

Jesus is the Word of God. He was before everything. He was and He is forever. Everything was made by Him and is being made now. For God is still making everything. From invisible things visible ones appear. God creates in this way and teaches us.

**Hebrew 11:3
By faith we understand that the worlds were framed by the word of God, so that the things which are seen were not made of things which are visible.

If the Word was in the beginning, let us look at that beginning? Let us see how God made visible things from invisible ones.

**Genesis 1:1-4
1. In the beginning God created the heavens and the earth.
2. The earth was without form, and void; and darkness was on the face of the deep. And the Spirit of God was hovering over the face of the waters.
3. Then God said, "Let there be light"; and there was light.
4. And God saw the light, that it was good; and God divided the light from the darkness.

The light was good. Everything that God had made was good. He has a lot of good words which we, as children of God, can use to create with.

**Genesis 1:6,9,11
6. Then God said, "Let there be a firmament in the midst of the waters, and let it divide the waters from the waters."
9. Then God said, "Let the waters under the heavens be gathered together into one place, and let the dry land appear"; and it was so.
11. Then God said, "Let the earth bring forth grass, the herb that yields seed, and the fruit tree that yields fruit according to its kind, whose seed is in itself, on the earth"; and it was so.

Then God said...
Then God said...
Then God said... and it was so.

If we need healing, we must turn to the word of healing. It is good to be saturated with this word like a litmus paper. We must meditate and speak this word until our faith starts working. When this word roots and germinates like a seed, it will become visible. The word will become the flesh. It is a mystery. There is nothing hidden which will not be revealed.

****Mark 4:22,23,26-28*
22. For there is nothing hidden which will not be revealed, nor has anything been kept secret but that it should come to light.
23. If anyone has ears to hear, let him hear."
26. And He said, "The kingdom of God is as if a man should scatter seed on the ground,
27. and should sleep by night and rise by day, and the seed should sprout and grow, he himself does not know how.
28. For the earth yields crops by itself: first the blade, then the head, after that the full grain in the head.

Without sowing we cannot reap. We cannot reap our health unless we sow the word of healing.

****John 1:3*
All things were made through Him, and without Him nothing was made that was made.

Jesus Christ is our almighty Doctor. He prescribes the medicine – His Word. His Word heals.

****Psalm 107:20*
He sent His word and healed them, And delivered them from their destructions.

****Psalm 103:3-5*
3. Who forgives all your iniquities, Who heals all your diseases,

4. Who redeems your life from destruction, Who crowns you with loving kindness and tender mercies,
5. Who satisfies your mouth with good things, So that your youth is renewed like the eagle's.

**Psalm 124:7
Our soul has escaped as a bird from the snare of the fowlers; The snare is broken, and we have escaped.

God heals all our diseases. The word "all" means all. Terminal diseases included. He redeemed our life from destruction. It is not necessary to die of illnesses. How do people die? Those who belong to Jesus and know His will do not die of sickness and disease. While they are living on this earth, their health is renewed as the word of God penetrates into their soul. Their health is renewed, for it is written: "Your youth is renewed like the eagle's."

Instead of growing old and decrepit from illnesses, the children of God live satisfied with their good and long life until old age, and then go home to their Father-God.

Death does not come to claim them. Instead, angels come to take them into the eternal life. Until then, we dwell in the secret place of the Most High.

**Psalm 91:1-6, 15, 16
1. He who dwells in the secret place of the Most High Shall abide under the shadow of the Almighty.
2. I will say of the LORD, "He is my refuge and my fortress; My God, in Him I will trust."
3. Surely He shall deliver you from the snare of the fowler And from the perilous pestilence.
4. He shall cover you with His feathers, And under His wings you shall take refuge; His truth shall be your shield and buckler.
5. You shall not be afraid of the terror by night, Nor of the arrow that flies by day,
6. Nor of the pestilence that walks in darkness, Nor of the destruction that lays waste at noonday.

15. He shall call upon Me, and I will answer him; I will be with him in trouble; I will deliver him and honor him.
16. With long life I will satisfy him, And show him My salvation."

Tell me, what else could we wish for? This is the word of God that guarantees us safety. Long life. Salvation. This is His promise of protection. Even in the very epicenter of disasters, destructions and epidemics we remain safe, because God is with us and at any moment He is ready to save. When does it happen? When we speak aloud, we release the word that is living and powerful. It always achieves its purpose.

**Hebrew 4:12*
For the word of God is living and powerful, and sharper than any two-edged sword, piercing even to the division of soul and spirit, and of joints and marrow, and is a discerner of the thoughts and intents of the heart.

**Isaiah 55:11*
So shall My word be that goes forth from My mouth; It shall not return to Me void, But it shall accomplish what I please, And it shall prosper in the thing for which I sent it.

For what purpose did God sent His word of healing? So that it would actually heal. The living word revives everything. How does it work in us? We put the living word into our mouth and confess it. "To confess" means to speak what the word of God says. According to Psalm 91 we say to God: "He is my refuge and my fortress; My God, in Him I will trust."
3 Surely He shall deliver you from the snare of the fowler And from the perilous pestilence.

"The perilous pestilence" in synodal translation of the Bible means wound, illness, epidemic, disaster. God says: "I deliver". By confessing this, by speaking it out loud, we in turn, bring this word into our physical world, because our problems are in physical dimension. All diseases, pain, fear, grief... exist here on the earth. However the truth is that God destroyed all these things on the Cross of Calvary.

If we trust in God and His word and release this word with our mouths it becomes a living word. We change the actual physical situation. We take it and change its course toward life. We create an absolutely different situation "while we do not look at the things which are seen, but at the things which are not seen. For the things which are seen are temporary, but the things which are not seen are eternal." (2 Corinthians 4:18)

The things which are seen are temporary. God teaches us not to dwell on visible things. He teaches us to grab a physical hold of all the promises which belong to us from the invisible world. Do not look at the thermometer, do not look at the visible tumour... It is temporary. It needs to change. Speak the word and change the situation! Know God's will for you. His will is your healing. Search the Scripture for every word that serves as proof, and proclaim it until your body becomes according to this word.

Without the word nothing was made.

From the book " Ever increasing faith " by Smith Wigglesworth,
chapter 4, page 39
I believe the Word of God is so powerful that it can change the life
of every person. There is a power in the Word of God which makes
things that are not as though they were. There is a creative power in
the word which comes from His mouth.

Speak, speak, speak, speak the healing words into your life. When you pronounce these words they attract the power of the Holy Spirit like a magnet. Your body reacts to the word of life with its every cell. It submits to the word of God. It was proved by scientific research. I want to tell you the story of one of God's generals at the turn of the XIX-XX centuries.

From the book "The diary of God's general" by John G. Lake
(chapter 1, page 16)
...Once I went through a number of tests. It was not enough for me
to know that God heals. I want to know how He does it.
I went to the experimental institute to go through a number of tests.
At first they connected a device to my head. It had a sensor which fixed
vibration of my brain.

I started repeating in my mind something like Psalm 23 to calm down my brain and make its vibration low. Then I repeated Psalm 31, Isaiah chapter 35, Psalm 91 and Paul's accusation of Agrippa... praying in my heart that God would anoint my soul by the Holy Spirit at some psychological moment. But recalling the texts I could not hold the Spirit that descended on me...

...When I said the last lines of verses, suddenly the Spirit of God filled me with a surge of praise and tongues. The pointer of the sensor reached the limit, and I had no idea how far it could go.

The professor said: "We have never seen anything like that... You are a phenomenon. You have the widest mental range of all people we have ever seen".

...I answered: "Gentlemen, this is the Holy Spirit".

During the second test a high-powered X-ray apparatus with a microscope was connected to my head. The aim was to see (if it is possible) the reaction of my brain cells.

I kept doing the same thing as I had done the previous time...As a result, when I stopped, the Spirit moved away. The professor said: "We cannot understand why, but the cells of cerebral cortex have utterly enlarged".

I told them: "Gentlemen, I want you to see something else. Go to the hospital and bring the man who has an inflammation of his bones. Take this device and connect to his leg. Leave enough room so that I could hold his leg...

When the device was already on, I put my hand on the man's leg and prayed...

I said: "God, kill this devilish disease with Your Power. Let the Holy Spirit work in him and live in him".

Then I asked: "Gentlemen, what is going on?" They answered: "The very cell is reacting".

This is very simple: the life of God comes back to the very affected little part of the body, the blood circulates immediately, overloaded cells react, and... the work has been done! This is the divine science of God.

Oh, my beloved, when you pray, something goes on! It is not a myth, it is an action of God.

I reread many times these discoveries by John G. Lake. It sobered me up from my former primitive mentality of the flesh. I began putting those principles to practice.

Once a wonderful lovely young woman from Moscow and I were standing together in a joint prayer for her husband's life. At that moment his body was reduced to a heap of bones covered with skin with a huge tumour on his stomach, but she decided not to accept the diagnosis of the last phase of cancer in her husband's body.

It seemed like the situation was getting worse and worse. He started feeling severe pain. We came together in prayer almost every evening and used the principles we had learned from "The diary of God's general". Laying her hands on the sick body of her husband, the woman addressed the tumour and proclaimed the Word of healing. She quoted with authority the verses from Ezekiel, chapter 37 and prophesied to the dry bones.

> ****Ezekiel 37:4-6**
> *4. Again He said to me, "Prophesy to these bones, and say to them, 'O dry bones, hear the word of the LORD! 5 Thus says the Lord GOD to these bones: "Surely I will cause breath to enter into you, and you shall live. 6 I will put sinews on you and bring flesh upon you, cover you with skin and put breath in you; and you shall live. Then you shall know that I am the LORD."'"*

We were also standing firm on the following Scriptures:

> ****1 Corinthians 7:4**
> *The wife does not have authority over her own body, but the husband does. And likewise the husband does not have authority over his own body, but the wife does*

It gave the understanding of her power over the body of her husband. And one more verse:

> ****Hebrew 11:35**
> *35. Women received their dead raised to life again. Others were tortured, not accepting deliverance, that they might obtain a better resurrection...*

We were spending time in these prayers, and unbelievable things began to happen. The tumour began receding. It became evident to everyone, including very competent doctors who were involved. A little bit later the man's gullet resumed its function, then the appetite returned...

The doctors were pumping out the liquid from his lungs, but his breathing was still labored. That is why the understanding came: she needs to address the lungs!.. and other internal organs!.. Even today the Word becomes flesh.

God teaches us this way.

I want to say that I saw that man in a different state, when after prayer his disease first abated. When we first met in Kiev, he said: "I have cancer. I have already been to Tibet. What do I do now?" We knelt before the true God.

A different life began in their family. His wife went to study at the Bible institute. The Word of God was proclaimed in their house... The disease was retreating...

It is so important for US not to abandon the Healer at the first sign of relief. It is easy to bustle around and to lose full dependence on the Source of our healing! The smallest deviation from the course can lead a plane to deviate from the flight path and ultimately miss the point of no return... The same applies to divine healing.

If you are not spiritually strong stay away from your old life style.

Just as without Jesus nothing was made that was made, nothing can be continued without Him as well. It is impossible to desire healing from God without being intimate with Him, without surrendering our body, mind and spirit to God. If you cannot humble your flesh and desires that are against the law of the Spirit of life (and we cannot do it by ourselves) we should seek the deliverance in God. We cannot do it without Jesus Christ and the Word of God. All things are made through Him. The Word heals. The Word delivers. We are sanctified by the Word. If we let the Word do His job, the disease stops its work in turn. If we make allowance for sin or weakness, we open the door and invite diseases and physical weaknesses. You cannot invite the Holy Spirit into your life, let Him settle in your body like in a temple, and at the same time keep in the portico or in the courtyard of this temple the trash of this world. We must simply make the decision to refuse to live according to the secular laws. The rest is Jesus' job. He makes us strong in our sickness. "Without Him — there is nothing ..."

Once I was on holiday in Crimea. As I was staying with a close friend the word spread that I was a cancer survivor . One day a very nice woman from a neighbouring village came to meet me. She was very lean with large thoughtful eyes, and a cancer diagnosis. It is difficult for intellectual and educated people to SIMPLY believe, but God touched her heart and she repented and accepted God that warm summer evening, was baptized by the Holy Spirit, began speaking in tongues. Her grayish complexion turned into a healthy flesh-coloured one. The Lord healed her. When saying goodbye she promised me to read the Bible every day.

I returned there a year later. I learned that at first everything had been great with her. She got visibly better and stronger, began gaining weight... But recovery was not enough. The most important thing was to stay alive...

The woman's cancer returned, but the faith, which was necessary to resist the disease, did not get stronger. The cancer proved stronger than her faith. I met her after she's had multiple surgeries. She understood everything: "I left God.", she said. "It was easy. Not to read the Bible one day, then you suddenly do not have time for it the next day... Day after day it becomes easier not to read God's Word and more difficult to come back to it... I became busy with other things..." She asked God to forgive her. It was between her and God.

Only God knows how sincere we are with Him. Believe me, no matter how far you have backslidden or became deceived, the Loving Father will always come to meet you in order to heal you and make you clean. If it were not so, no one could be saved.

Are there any corners in your soul which you do not let God in? Is there anything what you leave for yourself and do not want to change? It is enough to stop opening your Bible each day and stop communicating with God (no time) to suddenly find yourself in a dangerous situation. Praise God, that He is long-suffering and merciful. When you face an insoluble or painful problem, the Lord will be there ahead of you to help you. And believe me, it would not be because of Him that you found yourself in difficulty in the first place. Your problem will be a consequence of your lack of protection. If you move away from God-your strength, the secret place of the Most High, Satan will most definitely use it. He is watching you whether you let him approach you.

When we fill ourselves with Jesus, abide in Him, stay close to Him, Satan cannot reach us. We let God guard us with His protection. As it was written in the book of Job:

**_Job 1:8-10_
8. Then the LORD said to Satan, "Have you considered My servant Job, that there is none like him on the earth, a blameless and upright man, one who fears God and shuns evil?"
9. So Satan answered the LORD and said, "Does Job fear God for nothing?
10. Have You not made a hedge around him, around his household, and around all that he has on every side? You have blessed the work of his hands, and his possessions have increased in the land.

Job was under God's protection. He was a blameless and upright man, one who fears God and shuns evil. He had a period of severe physical sufferings. It seemed that it was easier to die than to believe in salvation from God, but Job knew the hand of the One Who is strong to mend all things. Being without any support he continued to set his hopes upon God.

**_Job 19:25-27_
25. For I know that my Redeemer lives, And He shall stand at last on the earth;
26. And after my skin is destroyed, this I know, That in my flesh I shall see God,
27. Whom I shall see for myself, And my eyes shall behold, and not another. How my heart yearns within me!

I would repeat these verses through tears, over and over again, just as my body was disintegrating after chemo therapy. There were so many tears! They streamed down my face and into my mouth so I would squeeze these verses out through salty bubbles... and at that moment God was so close. So close!

Even when it seems that nothing is happening, it is not true. In the presence of God something is always happening. It is happening to you. Let Him comfort you, touch your heart. Let His Word grow in you, be revealed to you... Become a good soil for His Word (Mark, chapter 4). One day, after you dwell in Him and He dwells in you enough, He will speak to you from within. Oh, you will know with absolute certainty that the disease and you are incompatible. That is what faith is. You will take His word for it, and this word will live and be active in you powerfully.

When we trust the Word of God in spite of circumstances, in spite of what our eyes see, in spite of the diagnosis by your doctor, we stay strong. We go through hard times until we reach divine health. We stand on God's Word. The Word does His job in us, and what He started He will complete. We cannot but trust Him. We must submit to Him, for He does it for our own good. And then, all will be well not only with our health, but we will learn to live in victory over demons, diseases and death.

Say this prayer with me aloud.
Heavenly Father!
I believe that Your word is living and powerful. You confirm Your word in my life right now. You confirm it by healing my body and by re-newing my soul.

I will learn and I will dwell in Your Word that heals. I will seek Your presence every day. Do not let me forget or doubt even for one moment that my life and my breath are in Your hands alone. I know that I am nothing without You, but with You "everything is possible for him who believes". I am already not of this world with its curses and pain. I am in my God!

You are my salvation, my healing, the strength of my life! May Your Word be sowed in me like in a good soil, root in my heart and germinate like a seed! Feed me with Your Heavenly bread, my Lord, so that I could grow in strength of faith and in strength of spirit and withstand all diseases with their symptoms, for it is written: "Man does not live on bread alone, but every word that comes from the mouth of God". Thank You, my God, for everything that Your mighty healing Word fills me with! Amen!

Chapter 4

Medicine to all your flesh

Proverbs 4:20-22
20. My son, give attention to my words; Incline your ear to my sayings.
21. Do not let them depart from your eyes; Keep them in the midst of your heart;
22. For they are life to those who find them, And health to all their flesh.

Health to all their flesh. Or medicine to all their flesh (another translation of the Bible). One universal medicine to all our flesh!

When we are taking this medicine and submitting to God's laws, we receive true healing, which He prepared for us 2010 years ago, when "He gave His only begotten Son, that whoever believes in Him should not perish but have everlasting life".(**John 3:16)And by His stripes we are healed. It is written in the Bible(**1Peter 2:24, **Isaiah 53). We will not be able to understand it, but God created us in a way that we are able to believe in it.

Therefore, Jesus is our Doctor, and the Word of God is the medicine He uses (see **Proverbs 4:22). How does this medicine penetrate into us? Through two channels: our eyes and our ears.

"If anyone has ears to hear, let him hear."(**Mark 4:23, **Luke 8:15)

These channels are always open to receive information. Negative words and words of anxiety, fear, disbelief and idle chatter... bring destruction. The Word of God brings life. There is an expression: "Be careful what you look into". When you look into the living word it will penetrate you and infuse you with life.

God tells us not to dwell on the things that are visible.

"For the things which are seen are temporary, but the things which are not seen are eternal". (**2Corinthians 4:18).

What do the doctors usually say? They talk about things that God does not want us to dwell on. They declare, announce, describe the diagnosis in detail and put an educated signature in our medical history, testifying to Satan's work. Disease is a curse. All disease comes from the world that is ruled by Satan. But we do not belong to this world if we are born again, and Jesus is our Lord. "Surely He has borne our griefs and carried our sorrows..." (**Isaiah 53:4)."...by whose stripes you were healed."(**1Peter 2:24). Whose words are we going to believe?

Scientists are quite right when they say that our organism can protect itself and resist illnesses. But in order to withstand an incurable disease we need to have a revelation about "...the exceeding greatness of His power toward us who believe..." (**Ephesians 1:19)

I am in the body of Christ. In Him I am above any unhealthy situation, above any infirmity and disease, above any crisis, and any unsolvable problem. For I am in Him! No one will be able to steal me from His hand. I am a new creature in Jesus Christ. I am a child of the Almighty God and I know His will concerning my healing. I trust His Word. When I am certain of this, I no longer behave like someone who is trying to get healing. I behave myself as someone who has already been healed. In order to refuse medical treatment and prescription drugs, you should be absolutely certain, you should have a revelation that Lord Jesus is the only One who heals today. He heals from cancer, AIDS, schizophrenia. He raises from the dead. I was healed from cancer in 2005, and before that- from alcoholism, in 1999. God gave me new organs and I no longer take medications. When I got the revelation that by His stripes I was healed 2000 years ago, I refused medicine. Not because I did not feel the pain, but because I understood the truth. All other ways of seeking healing became senseless.

All this certainty did not happen right away, but as a result of a process, as the Word of God entered deeper and deeper into my heart. It is necessary to come to this point. Day after day, consistently and patiently I need to fill myself with the word of healing (if I am in need healing), with the word of prosperity (if I am having financial problems), with the word which guarantees the salvation of my children (when I pray for the salvation of my child). To be patient means to stay strong concerning what God's Word says about my situation. And one day my soul comes into agreement with the Word of God and the certainty in the invisible begins to work, the certainty that the healing belongs to me at this very moment. And then my body begins to obey that certainty. And the Word, God's medicine, dissolves within me and becomes flesh. It is a miracle. And it is a process as well.

Let the word of healing enter into your system, like medicine, until your mind comes into agreement with this word and then your body will conform to your certainty. It is always a process. As a rule it is a long process, but the only reliable one, because it is the prescription of God Himself.

Not everybody will agree to live according to such a prescription. It is easier for those people, who have already been refused by the doctors, as nothing more could be done for them, and the priests are quietly preparing the farewell requiem with the words, "Everything is God's will", while their exhausted relatives have lost all hope, having spent all family savings on medical treatments ...

**Mark 5:25-29
25. Now a certain woman had a flow of blood for twelve years,
26. and had suffered many things from many physicians. She had spent all that she had and was no better, but rather grew worse.
27. When she heard about Jesus, she came behind Him in the crowd and touched His garment.
28. For she said, "If only I may touch His clothes, I shall be made well."
29. Immediately the fountain of her blood was dried up, and she felt in her body that she was healed of the affliction.

Are you familiar with a situation like that? There is nothing new under the sky. It is easy for me to talk to such people. They are opened to impossible things, because all the possible things have already been tried and have either brought no result or made things worse.

Twenty-four hours a day I tell people about the principles of God's healing. I will never get tired of it. I know for certain that at the moment I am sharing the message of healing the Holy Spirit takes it up and puts into the mind of the listener. The word of healing gets to the listener through healing. It is not my work. It is the healing work of the Holy Spirit. It is the one true medicine that uproots the problem whatever it may be. The Word of God strikes into the root of the problem like a sword, in a completely different dimension. You may want to remove the consequence of the problem by trying to restore the stricken body with chemical remedies. But your body simply reflects that which is within you, your spirit. Spiritual problems can be solved only on a spiritual level.

It does not matter how long you try to exterminate cancer with chemotherapy or heat up your body from within to the critical temperature in an attempt to burn out cancer cells, you cannot force cancer to leave the body which it has occupied. When the spirit of cancer feels any discomfort, it can resurface in another part of the body. We call this occupied part metastases. Cancer is not threatened by temperature. It is a spirit. It will not leave the dwelling where it has settled. If this spirit is not satisfied with the territory of just your body, it will go on spreading onto your family and loved ones. Evil loves entering the metastases phase. This generational spreading is what we describe as a "family curse".

Behind every disease there is a spirit. To be more specific —a demon. Since your healing is not accomplished by a mere process "IT", but by a person —"HIM" (Jesus), you also need to understand that "cancer" is more than a term. It is a spirit which found its way into your body. There is a reason for it. Only you and God know the real reason. It does not have to be adultery, or any obvious transgression. The reason for cancer to gain access can be something as simple as a shallow understanding of the truth that you are a new creature in Jesus Christ and you possess His nature. No disease has a power to break into your body. However, if Satan manages to deceive you (it is his job on the earth, as he is a father of lies), and you do not resist his symptoms with strong faith, then he will start taking control your body with sickness until he becomes the sole possessor of it. That is why

**Acts 10:38*
"...God anointed Jesus of Nazareth with the Holy Spirit and with power, who went about doing good and healing all who were oppressed by the devil, for God was with Him."

And today God does His job through the Holy Spirit and our job is to resist the devil with strong faith.

**James 4:7*
"Therefore submit to God. Resist the devil and he will flee from you."

Your body is a dwelling place for the Holy Spirit.

***1Corinphians 3:16,17*
"Do you not know that you are the temple of God and that the Spirit of God dwells in you?
If anyone defiles the temple of God, God will destroy him. For the temple of God is holy, which temple you are."

***1Corinphians 6:19*
"Or do you not know that your body is the temple of the Holy Spirit who is in you, whom you have from God, and you are not your own?"

No other spirit can have a place in your body without your permission. Do not accept any diagnosis. Nourish your spirit with God's Word, strengthen yourself with faith so that you could resist with strong faith. Satan is watching your reactions. Your reaction must be: "I will not fear!"; "The One Who is in me is greater than the one who is in the world"; "No disaster will come near my tent!"

I want to share an instance out of my medical history pertaining to this illness (happened a while back). I was at home resting between sessions of the exhausting procedures at the oncology center. I was very weak during that time; slept a lot, ate almost nothing, the amount of chemicals in my system was so high that my body had no natural urges. It seemed like I was on a forced long-lasting fast. The medicine often provoked vomiting. When I was able to fall asleep, my soul rested a little. One day God let me see with my spiritual eyes what was really happening in the spiritual dimension. It was the manifestation of gifts of the Holy Spirit. I am so grateful to God for that moment, because it completely changed my attitude. I was about to wake up with my eyes half-open. I saw a face above me, which I will never forget. It was a man's face. His eyes were almost transparent and his hair was tangled. I knew for sure that it was a spirit of cancer. He did not look me in the eyes and turned away. He stood rigid above me. He was waiting for my reaction! God removed all fear from me. I was able to think clearly. My mind was being filled with the word from God. Why did this person have such entangled hair? Who usually has hair like that? Homeless people? What does that mean? A homeless person does not have rights to live in a specific house. He does not have a residence permit. Then I understood. This time I reacted according to the truth: Cancer! You are a homeless person, squatting in my body. You do not have any rights to stay in my body! My body is a dwelling place for the Holy Spirit! And where the Spirit of the Lord is, there is freedom.

It seemed like a mere moment. It was not a dream, because I saw the light from the windows through my eyelashes and heard my husband walking in the room...It took time for this truth, that God has just revealed to me, to root itself in my mind. Since that moment on, however, my attitude changed completely. I began fighting back.

It is impossible to receive the healing from God, while avoiding His prescription. His medicine is His Word. When you accept the Lord as your Doctor you must completely trust Him. It will be possible when you come to know Him as Someone Who will never let you down. Who is mighty to change any unhealthy situation in your body. Who will never leave you or forsake you. Who loved you so much, that He consented to be born in the flesh, in order to offer his body as a sacrifice for us and separate us from this world, so that this world would not be able to kill us with its diseases.

**Psalm 107:20
"He sent His word and healed them, And delivered them from their
destructions."

Your health has been paid for, yet you are still carrying around pain and suffering. Give yourself to God. Give Him your mind so that, He could occupy it, instead of letting it be filled with fear and depression. Give Him your body, and it will be no longer yours, but the body of Jesus.

> *From the book of John G. Lake "The power above demons, dis-*
> *eases and death" (chapter 9, page 87)*
> *I want you to understand that the dedication of your body, soul*
> *and spirit to God is very important. It means that you take yourself*
> *out of the hands of men and also the devil and place yourself into*
> *God's hands, thus making a strong decision to follow God's way and*
> *fulfill His will. Let us pretend that your spirit is ill. Where would you*
> *go to ease that kind of pain? You can go to spiritualists or mediums,*
> *but it will not be God's way of solving the problem.*
> *...When our spirit is ill, we must go to the Father of spirits. When*
> *our soul suffers, we go to the Lord. If we have problems within our*
> *body, who do we go to? Unfortunately most Christians today first*
> *seek help from the world, people and even the devil.*
> *...Do you really think that when you come to Heaven, you will*
> *see multitudes of people who depended on medications, various pre-*
> *scription drugs, nausea pills?*
> *The Talmud has a great prescription for healing— repeating*
> *Psalm 91 seven times a day. If a man repeated Psalm 91 seven times*
> *a day, the spirit of faith penetrated into his soul. It was known as*
> *good medicine for the soul and body.*

When you learn the Word of God and saturate your mind with it, your body will come to know it and accept the healing. Jesus is you healing. He, Jesus, is the Word of God, and He is the medicine for your body. In the presence of His healing power the presence of victory will come.

From the book "The Diary of God's General" by John G. Lake (chapter 1, page 22)

The presence of power and the presence of victory is the presence of dedication to God. This victory comes when a man clenches his teeth and says:"I am going this way, with God ".

There is not a man who can detect the operation of faith in a human heart.

But we can be absolutely sure that when we refrain from any other help, our Lord Jesus Christ will never let us down. When defeats happen, it is ours, but not God's.

Tell me, how much time you spend in medical offices and pharmacies in a quest for panacea? How much money is spent on medications, homeopathy, procedures and remuneration? Would it not be better to spend this time learning the truth about God's healing, which excludes everything that does not achieve a result, but only temporary relief? You can spend half of your life on the surgical table, and still not solve the problem. Even if, after the surgery, only one part of you remains, cancer will not hesitate to attack it! For it is written:

**John 10:10
"The thief does not come except to steal, and to kill, and to destroy. I have come that they may have life, and that they may have it more abundantly."

If your body does not reflect abundance, when it is healthy, fresh and viable, it means there is no truth. You need to do your best to learn the truth about yourself. This truth sets us free. It is better to learn the truth and accept the deliverance before it is too late.

When I recovered, I began looking for those to whom I could be a supporter. I met a woman who "had suffered many things from many physicians. She had spent all that she had and was no better, but rather grew worse" (**Mark 5:26). She was in the last phase of cancer. She was a believer, but she was in a critical condition. There was not a hair left on her head. She was suffering from pain. But in the church she attended people believed that "everything is in God's will". When she came to me for the first time doubling up from pain, I laid my hands upon her and prayed. To my unconcealed joy when she left she felt no pain. I visited her very often and talked to her on the phone. I did my best to be her supporter in her fight for life. But one day I went out of town and when I came back I found her in a horrible condition. She was screaming from pain. Her body had a putrid color. She could not even go to the toilet...

With God's help I was able to put her in the car and took her to the hospital where I personally knew the doctors. They performed an ultrasound test and I told me that she had two days to live at most. The metastases were everywhere. The process was irreversible, they said. By Monday she will be dead ...

I asked to keep her in the hospital until Monday and told the doctors:"Do your best, and God will do what He can!"

I do not know why I said those words, but the doctors left the room. God gave power to those words.

The doctors put her on a catheter and gave her painkillers. I was permitted to speak with her. I said: "Irina! You do not feel pain now. Let us take the true medicine for the whole body". And we opened the Bible, read it and proclaimed the words of healing. When I was leaving she was smiling. It was Saturday. On Sunday evening when I got into the ward, she did not recognize me. Her pupils were as big as her eyeballs and I understood that the death came as the competent doctors had predicted. They were not mistaken in terms. But at that moment I felt a great boldness rise in me! I seated her body on a bed and her head fell on her chest. I put my hands on her jugular vertebra (ask me why? I do not know) and recalled that wicked face with whitish eyes and tangled hair, and directed my words to the face. Where did this daring come from, my Lord? At that moment I commanded the cancer and death in the name and authority of Christ. And I had a reason: He who is in me is greater than he whom I addressed (1John 4:4 "You are of God, little children, and have overcome them, because He who is in you is greater than he who is in the world"). And suddenly she began to snore under my hands. I thought: "If she is snoring, she is sleeping; if she is sleeping, she is alive".

On Monday I received a call from the hospital. They said: "She wants to go home. Can we let her go?"

"Yes, you can"

"With catheter?"

"Yes, with catheter... What do you think of it?"

"It is inexplicable"

...Irina lived for about two months after that. She could live and live...Everything was so good in the beginning. God raised her from the dead. She removed the catheter, because she did not need it anymore. But time passed and the symptoms returned. With an increased speed cancer started making up for the time lost. I could not understand it. I prayed and asked God to explain to me what was wrong. I understood that God had nothing to do with that. He never takes His blessings from His children. Satan steals them.

**John 10:10
"The thief does not come except to steal, and to kill, and to destroy."

And God answered me: "The Word of God is not read in her house". Oh, my Lord! I rushed to call Irina: "You do not read the Word, do you?" And I heard the answer: "Irina, I am so tired".

Tell me, which one of us can choose how long we get to live on this earth? Who chooses what medications and how much we can take? Who has that choice?

Having walked through the valley of the shadow of death with God, having taken (Can four years of cancer-free life, without doctors and drugs be considered a result?), I can only help you learn how to take His medicine. But I cannot take it for you. At the first symptoms of disease, take His vaccine for the whole body. Take preventive measures according to God's method. It is absolutely different from all the methods you have ever tried, but it is the most profitable method of all which has ever existed. You do not need to spend money for it. It does not have any side effects. All you invest is your time, which you spend with God. You can get much more than you can possibly imagine.

**Joshua 1:8
"This Book of the Law shall not depart from your mouth, but you shall meditate in it day and night, that you may observe to do according to all that is written in it. For then you will make your way prosperous, and then you will have good success."

Fill you mind with the Word of God, and radiation of the Holy Spirit will destroy pathogenic microbes. The Word of God, like a mixture, will penetrate into you (through eyes and ears) and perform its healing.

This process must be constant. Constancy always has power. If you can keep up with this way of life, nothing will be impossible for you. You will be invulnerable to diseases.

Having written this chapter I must also say the following:
**I am not against painkillers;
**I am not against doctors;
**I am not calling for action to rid the world of hospitals;
**I AM for focusing your hope on God, who gives life to the dead... and even more so to those who are sick...

...And then not only the heavenly anaesthesia will do its work in you, but also His truth and the law of the spirit of life in Jesus Christ.

From the book of John G. Lake "The power above demons, diseases and death" (page 49, chapter 5)

In Exodus chapter 15 we find a covenant of healing which God has made with the people of Israel after they had crossed the Red Sea and came to Marah. The Almighty Lord made that covenant with them as Jehovah-Rafa, which means "Lord-Healer". God's people lived for many years under that covenant. Israel did not have doctors for centuries. People of different social origin, rich and poor, kings and servants set their hopes upon the Living and Eternal God. There is only one occurrence in the Bible when a man broke the covenant with God - Asa, the King of Judah. He suffered from a disease in his feet, but he did not trust God and sought the help of physicians, and therefore came to rest with his fathers.

**2Chronicles 16:12,13
"And in the thirty-ninth year of his reign, Asa became diseased in his feet, and his malady was severe; yet in his disease he did not seek the LORD, but the physicians.   So Asa rested with his fathers; he died in the forty-first year of his reign."

The most remarkable words about healing belong to King David:

**Psalm 105:37
"He also brought them out with silver and gold, and there was none feeble among His tribes."

Think about all this...
And say this prayer with me aloud.
Heavenly Father!
I open my heart so that I could receive from You the prescription for my healing. Let my heart be a spacious storage for Your healing words and a treasure house for all the days of my life.

Help me, Lord, to be faithful in nourishing myself with Your Word and not to be unfaithful in what You teach me. Help me to put my hope in You as my personal Healer. I attune my ear to Your Word to hear the very word that will make me healthy and whole. In the name of Jesus!
Amen!

Chapter 5

Do not be afraid!

**Luke 8:41,42*
And behold, there came a man named Jairus, and he was a ruler of the synagogue. And he fell down at Jesus' feet and begged Him to come to his house, for he had an only daughter about twelve years of age, and she was dying.

**Luke 8:49,50*
While He was still speaking, someone came from the ruler of the synagogue's house, saying to him, "Your daughter is dead. Do not trouble the Teacher." But when Jesus heard it, He answered him, saying, "Do not be afraid; only believe, and she will be made well.

These words were spoken to the man whose daughter had already died. It was a serious cause to get depressed. There was every reason to doubt Jesus' words. But the faith of that man saved him. He did not turn back to bury his daughter. He followed Jesus. He trusted in His words. And his daughter rose from the dead. Is there anything impossible for God?

What requirements were there in order to resurrect the dead girl? Jesus made no stipulations. He only required two things. "Do not be afraid!" — was the first. "Only believe!" — was the second.

It is with good reason that God so often gives us the same instruction: Do not fear! Be strong and of good courage! Do not be afraid, nor be dismayed!

> ****_Joshua 1:6,7,9_**
> *"Be strong and of good courage, for to this people you shall divide as an inheritance the land which I swore to their fathers to give them. Only be strong and very courageous, that you may observe to do according to all the law which Moses My servant commanded you; do not turn from it to the right hand or to the left, that you may prosper wherever you go.*
> *Have I not commanded you? Be strong and of good courage; do not be afraid, nor be dismayed, for the LORD your God is with you wherever you go."*

Surely, the fear comes. But God does not move away. Your faith must be certain of it at all times.

> ****_Hebrews 13:5,6_**
> *"For He Himself has said, "I will never leave you nor forsake you.*
> *So we may boldly say: " The LORD is my helper; I will not fear. What can man do to me?"*

> ****_Isaiah 44:8_**
> *"Do not fear, nor be afraid; have I not told you from that time, and declared it? You are My witnesses. Is there a God besides Me? Indeed there is no other Rock; I know not one.'"*

The almighty God is always with you. You should not be afraid! It might seem that everything is being destroyed, that you are dying, and the situation is about to become irreversible...If Satan tries to impose disease, destruction or any other curse upon you, do not agree with it. Do not react, do not respond to it. He will make you think that God gave up on you, that you will never overcome this situation. It is a lie. Satan is a liar! His tactics are meant to frighten and deceive you. Just stay strong while God completes His work within you, until you are able to withstand with strong faith.

From the book "Pursuit of His Presence" by Kenneth and Gloria Copeland (January the 27th)
...Faith is the power which God uses to create. Fear is the power which devil uses to destroy.
...Your boundary of fear is your boundary of defeat. Where the fear starts faith stops. It takes courage to cross the boundary of this fear, to move the fear farther and farther away until "I am not afraid" becomes real in your life.

If your illness was diagnosed as incurable, and you think that you cannot resist, the Bible says that we can have control over the fear in our life. We need to know this and declare our authority, by saying:"Fear, I rebuke you in the name of Jesus. Doubt, I rebuke you in the name of Jesus!". Doubt and fear will leave you when you do so.

**1Timothy 1:7
"For God has not given us a spirit of fear, but of power and of love and of a sound mind."

Fear is a spirit. Cancer is a spirit. God has given us power, and the One who is in us is greater... The Holy Spirit is greater, above all, and He lets us triumph in His victory.

From the book of John G. Lake "The power above demons, diseases and death" (chapter 12 page 114-119).
The law of fear works in the physical world as well as in spiritual one. A man lives in fear. For example, someone is ill with typhus, and there is a warning sign on his house which is put to prevent the spread of disease. Fear puts you under control. When your mind is full of fear, pores of your body inhale everything that surrounds you. This is how people are infected with diseases.
...Pay attention how this law works. Faith is the basis of this law. Faith is the direct opposite of fear, so it has an opposite effect in man's spirit, soul and body. Faith makes man's spirit become confident, and it makes man's mind become calm — his thoughts become positive. A positive mind rejects the disease. Therefore, the radiation of the Holy

Spirit destroys pathogenic microbes...When a man consciously makes himself be in touch with God, the faith captures his heart and changes his nature. Instead of being afraid a man is filled with faith. Instead of attracting any illnesses his spirit resists any of them. The Spirit of Jesus Christ fills this man — his hands, his heart, every cell of his body.

Once I was ministering in the area where bubonic plague was rife and rampant. It was impossible to find any people willing to bury the dead even for hundreds of dollars. But I was not infected... We buried the people who died from bubonic plague... Because we knew that the law of life in Jesus Christ protected us. This law worked.

The governmental ship with medicines and a team of doctors was sent to help victims. One of doctors asked me: "What did you use to protect yourself? Our team has different preventive means, and we are sure that if you could stay healthy serving the sick and burying the dead, you have some secret. What is it?"

I answered: "Brother, my secret is the law of the Spirit of life in Jesus Christ. I believe that while my soul is in touch with Living God and His Spirit, which can flow into my soul and body, not even one microbe will be able to stick to me, for the Holy Spirit will kill it". He asked: "Do you not think, that you should be inoculated?" I answered: "I do not think so. But if you want to experiment on me, you can take foam from one of the dead and examine it with a microscope. You will see a mass of living microbes. You will realize that they stay alive for a long time after human death. Put them on my hand which I will put under the microscope and you will see that the microbes will die at once instead of being alive". They did what I said and saw evidence that I was right. "How could it happen?" they asked, surprised. I answered: "It the law of the Spirit of life in Jesus Christ in action. When man's spirit and body are filled with a blessed presence of God, His Spirit exudes through pores of your body and kills microbes".

I think this information is exhaustive. I could conclude this chapter right here.

There are several books that I always keep by my side. This passage is from one of them. What sort of information do you fill yourself with? This determines whether you will be led by fear or faith. There is also a stream of information that we absorb on a regular basis which is purely trivial and devoid of any real substance or pertinance. These useless facts do not bring life, but occupy the place within us which should instead be filled with the Word of God that brings faith.

One day we will be weighed. And found... People who fill themselves with this world will be filled with fear and emptiness.

**Daniel 5:27
"...You have been weighed in the balances, and found wanting;"

Chapter 11 of the Book of Hebrews is a chapter about exploits of faith and people of faith

"...who through faith subdued kingdoms, worked righteousness, obtained promises, stopped the mouths of lions, quenched the violence of fire, escaped the edge of the sword, out of weakness were made strong, became valiant in battle, turned to flight the armies of the aliens. Women received their dead raised to life again. Others were tortured, not accepting deliverance, that they might obtain a better resurrection."(**Hebrew 11:33-35)

Because of weakness we are made strong. It means we have some strengthening to do. According to the Word of God we can resist the devil only with strong faith.

**Peter 5:9
"Resist him, steadfast in the faith..."

With strong faith...You need to nourish your faith, fill it up and nourish it again until it forces out fear and anxiety. So that only peace will remain. Who has peace today? He who dwells in the secret place of the Most High.

**Psalm 91
1. He who dwells in the secret place of the Most High Shall abide under the shadow of the Almighty.
2. I will say of the LORD, "He is my refuge and my fortress; My God, in Him I will trust."

3. Surely He shall deliver you from the snare of the fowler[a] And from the perilous pestilence.

4. He shall cover you with His feathers, And under His wings you shall take refuge; His truth shall be your shield and buckler.

5. You shall not be afraid of the terror by night, Nor of the arrow that flies by day,

6. Nor of the pestilence that walks in darkness, Nor of the destruction that lays waste at noonday.

7. A thousand may fall at your side, And ten thousand at your right hand; But it shall not come near you.

8. Only with your eyes shall you look, And see the reward of the wicked.

9. Because you have made the LORD, who is my refuge, Even the Most High, your dwelling place,

10. No evil shall befall you, Nor shall any plague come near your dwelling;

11. For He shall give His angels charge over you, To keep you in all your ways.

12. In their hands they shall bear you up, Lest you dash your foot against a stone.

13. You shall tread upon the lion and the cobra, The young lion and the serpent you shall trample underfoot.

14. "Because he has set his love upon Me, therefore I will deliver him; I will set him on high, because he has known My name.

15. He shall call upon Me, and I will answer him; I will be with him in trouble; I will deliver him and honor him.

16. With long life I will satisfy him, And show him My salvation."

It seems that everyone is familiar with this psalm. In this message God promises to protect those who choose the Lord as their refuge, fortress and hope.

Verse 5: "You shall not be afraid..." We will not have fear only if we dwell in the secret place of the Most High. To make this secret place real we need to abide in Him.

**John 15:7
"If you abide in Me, and My words abide in you, you will ask what you desire, and it shall be done for you."

And then

> ****_Isaiah 54:14,15,17_**
> *14. In righteousness you shall be established; You shall be far from op-*
> *pression, for you shall not fear; And from terror, for it shall not come*
> *near you.*
> *15. Indeed they shall surely assemble, but not because of Me. Whoever*
> *assembles against you shall fall for your sake.*
> *17. No weapon formed against you shall prosper,*

When we strive for His presence, seek intimacy with Him, abide in His Word, nourish our spirit (our inner human) from His Spirit, He who is Love forces out any fear.

> ****_1John 4:18_**
> *"There is no fear in love; but perfect love casts out fear, because fear in-*
> *volves torment. But he who fears has not been made perfect in love."*

We can reach perfection. He presented Himself to us as the Word, which creates, changes and corrects everything... God gives us instructions:

> ****_Joel 3:10_ *"Let the weak say, 'I am strong.'"*

Then let the timorous say: "I will not be afraid!" (**Psalm 90), let the weak say: "I will never be uprooted!" (**Proverbs 10:30), let the sick say: "By His stripes I am healed!!!" (1 Peter 2:24)...

Faith is strengthened with the Word. Through the Word we are healed. Through the Word we are created in His image from faith to faith.

When I was told that there is cancer in my body and my parents were clearly notified that: "It is over", the most surprising thing was that there was no feeling of terrifying panic. In some unintelligible way the fear moved away. Later, during the hard times I experienced everything: pain, weakness, sorrow..., but there was no fear! There was even a moment when I felt I was leaving my body, but even then I felt no fear. I was not a slave to fear. I could feel that it was not in me. I felt God's presence. God drew close to me to lead me out of "the valley of the shadow of death". My husband, Dmitry, always came into my ward with a big smile on his face. The doctor once asked us whether we understood the gravity of our situation... Meanwhile I knew that I was in the secret place of the Most High. Even when my eyes could only see the four walls of the terrible bunker, where a thick lead door separated me from air and light, where radioactive irradiation was turned on my cancer-affected body, I was concealed in the secret place of the Most High. And since I did not eat anything, but only prayed all the time, the line between this world and the next was hardly present, and I saw in my spirit that, every time when I was put under the killing radioactive rays, that the Lord created His own shelter and held my head with His hands standing next to the head of the bed. He was right there with me. He did not leave me nor forsake me. His promises remained.

**<u>Isaiah 43:2</u>
"When you pass through the waters, I will be with you; And through the rivers, they shall not overflow you. When you walk through the fire, you shall not be burned, Nor shall the flame scorch you."

In the visible world I seemed to be burned, but the flame did not scorch me! How was this possible? Through my God! How mighty You are in Your Word! I had to undergo one particular procedure when an electrode was placed into my body, proceeding to heat up everything inside to extreme temperature. The nurses put ice all around me so that I would not burn out completely. Living cells in my body were being burned away along with the cancerous ones. How can one survive such an ordeal? How is it possible that today all of my organs are functioning? My husband was told: "Take her home, she will not be able to stand it any longer. Go and file for disability".

Abraham did not acknowledge himself childless. He saw Himself as a father of many nations. Sarah gave birth to a son at the age of 90. We are children of Abraham according to our faith, when we follow Christ. I did not acknowledge myself an invalid. I trusted in God Who raises from the dead. And today I say: "I have new organs! All my internal organs are functioning according to the law of the spirit of life in Jesus Christ! This is the fact!"

The Lord Jesus disabled the fear in me. Cancer could no longer spread through my body. I could panic every time when I felt new and unexpected symptoms, but Jesus was always near, and fear gave up. He Who is in me was always greater then the visible circumstance.

**Philippians 1:28*
"...and not in any way terrified by your adversaries, which is to them a proof of perdition, but to you of salvation, and that from God."

**Psalm 27:1-3*
1. The LORD is my light and my salvation; Whom shall I fear? The LORD is the strength of my life; Of whom shall I be afraid?
2. When the wicked came against me To eat up my flesh, y enemies and foes, They stumbled and fell.
3. Though an army may encamp against me, My heart shall not fear; Though war may rise against me, In this I will be confident.

My adversary was cancer, but not only that. My adversaries were doubt, lack of faith, ignorance and everything else that separated me from the truth, the Word of God. But they stumbled and fell! God is always the same. He does not change. Am I the first who had to go through excrutiating treatments of radioactive irradiation and chemical poisoning? According to all laws of nature, when the human body becomes disabled, one becomes an invalid. But when God's mighty arm is with us the laws of nature take a step back. If it is in God's will to change the laws, to turn them back, to stop the moon and the sun, to move the shadow ten steps back... He does it. He is God. And He is OUR God.

In the book of prophet Daniel there is a story about three young men devoted to God, who did not fall down and worship the golden idol and for that were thrown into a blazing furnace. They trusted in God Who would never leave or forsake them. They trusted in Him when they were threatened with death, they trusted in Him when were thrown into the furnace, they trusted in Him when they were already in the furnace.

**_Daniel 3:27_
"And the satraps, administrators, governors, and the king's counsel-
ors gathered together, and they saw these men on whose bodies the
fire had no power; the hair of their head was not singed nor were their
garments affected, and the smell of fire was not on them."

Those young men were human like us. Prophet Elijah was just like us. Apostle Paul was just like us. As the Spirit of the Living God was with them, He is with us today and He covers us with His clothes, makes the flame harmless, preserves the hair on our head - "and the smell of fire was not on them". Reading their story in the Bible, I understood that with our Eternal God everyone lives.

Day by day, month by month, the Lord taught me through His Word and through the Holy Spirit, so that my youth was renewed like the eagle's (**Psalm 103:5). God stopped cancer with His Word. He prohibited death. He is the in Charge of life.

**_Proverbs 3:21-27_
21. My son, let them not depart from your eyes — Keep sound wisdom
and discretion;
22. So they will be life to your soul And grace to your neck.
23. Then you will walk safely in your way, And your foot will not stum-
ble.
24. When you lie down, you will not be afraid; Yes, you will lie down
and your sleep will be sweet.
25. Do not be afraid of sudden terror, Nor of trouble from the wicked
when it comes;
26. For the LORD will be your confidence, And will keep your foot
from being caught.
27. Do not withhold good from those to whom it is due, When it is in
the power of your hand to do so.

You know, my body would have fought off the disease much faster had I been stronger in trusting God and His truth. The knowledge of this truth set me free from the incurable disease. What truth? The truth that God redeemed me from sickness and disease 2000 years ago.

The healing belongs to me. I had to spend time with the Word of God to learn it. Before, I had not spent enough time with God to equip me with strong faith for a bad day. A bad day came, but my faith was not strong enough. Spend the time today to learn the truth that you are free from any weakness and disease of any kind. Do it NOW! Do not expect the tumour to resolve by itself just because you are Christian. Do not expect that your child will grow up and turn away from this sinful world by himself. We need to know through our spirit that:

> ****<u>Isaiah 54:13</u>**
> **"All your children shall be taught by the LORD, And great shall be the peace of your children."**

Then, if any destructive circumstances invade your life, you will be ready to take them on with the power of the Holy Spirit and the Word of faith. The first words which you will proclaim with your mouth into this world:

I WILL NOT BE AFRAID! Fear, I rebuke you in the name of Jesus. Doubt, I rebuke you in the name of Jesus! For God is with me.

Pray with me according to Psalm 91.

He is my refuge and my fortress; my God, in Him I will trust. Surely He will deliver me from the snare of the fowler and from the perilous pestilence. He will cover me with His feathers, and under His wings I will take refuge; His truth will be my shield and buckler. I will not be afraid of the terror by night, nor of the arrow that flies by day, nor of the pestilence that walks in darkness, nor of the destruction that lays waste at noonday. A thousand may fall at my side, and ten thousand at my right hand; but it will not come near me. Because I have made the LORD, who is my refuge, even the Most High, my dwelling place, no evil will befall me, nor will any plague come near my dwelling; for He will give His angels charge over me, to keep me in all my ways. In their hands they will bear me up, lest I dash my foot against a stone. I will tread upon the lion and the cobra, the young lion and the serpent I will

trample underfoot. I will call upon Him, and He will answer me; He will be with me in trouble; He will deliver me and honor me. With long life He will satisfy me, and show me His salvation."
Amen!

Chapter 6

Only believe!

**Luke 8:41,42
*41. And behold, there came a man named Jairus, and he was a ruler
of the synagogue. And he fell down at Jesus' feet and begged Him to
come to his house,*
*42. for he had an only daughter about twelve years of age, and she
was dying.*

**Luke 8:49,50
*49. While He was still speaking, someone came from the ruler of the
synagogue's house, saying to him, "Your daughter is dead. Do not trouble
the Teacher."*
*50. But when Jesus heard it, He answered him, saying, "Do not be afraid;
only believe, and she will be made well.".*

**Mark 9:23
*"Jesus said to him, "If you can believe, all things are possible to him
who believes."*

**John 11:40
*"Jesus said to her, "Did I not say to you that if you would believe you
would see the glory of God?"*

Jesus said to him, Jesus said to her... Jesus is saying the same to you today: "Do not be afraid; only believe!" His word is still temporal, living and active, because He is still the same, nothing changes in Him and He is creating everything even today.

Does He not tell us in His Word that if we believe, we will see His glory? We will see the wounds heal, the pain move away, and death back down when the law of the spirit of life in Jesus Christ is put into action (**Romans 8:2; **John 11:40). Surely we will see it. God's condition is for us to believe.

> *From the book of Kenneth E. Hagin "The basics of spiritual growth (Chapter 1 "How do we receive the faith?")*
>
> *If God required faith from us when it is impossible for us to have it, we would have a right to complain. But if He gives us the actual source of faith, then having faith and putting it to practice becomes our responsibility.*
>
> *...To blame God for our own lack of faith is ignorance. God prepared the way by which faith is accessible to all.*

**Hebrews 11:6
"But without faith it is impossible to please Him, for he who comes to God must believe that He is, and that He is a rewarder of those who diligently seek Him."

He rewards us by His healing. He is ready to fulfill all our needs. We must be prepared to receive his blessings. The only way to receive them from God is by faith.

You cannot become a giant of faith for 24 hours. It is a personal spiritual journey that lasts a lifetime.

**Hebrews 11:1-3
"Now faith is the substance of things hoped for, the evidence of things not seen.
For by it the elders obtained a good testimony. By faith we understand that the worlds were framed by the word of God, so that the things which are seen were not made of things which are visible."

The entire 11th chapter of the Book of Hebrews is about faith and heroic deeds of faith. Nothing has changed since then. If we dare to live by faith today, there will be no end of miracles. Elijah was just like us. The people described in chapter11 had the same measure of faith as we have today. Those people believed in miracles and lived by them, because they trusted in God.

One of the brightest examples of this is the story of Job. Being the most prosperous and wealthy man of the East he suffered a terrible destruction in his life. He lost everything except his hope and trust in God.

**_Job 19:25_
"For I know that my Redeemer lives..."

**_Romans 10:10_
"For with the heart one believes unto righteousness, and with the mouth confession is made unto salvation."

We believe with our hearts. Faith and certainty reside in the heart. How do they get there? When we plant the Word of God into our heart. We are filled with the Word by the way of our eyes and ears. We become filled to the point of overflowing...The living word starts living within us. It does its work within us. And then it begins to speak to us. We hear God from within. We begin to believe. This is the moment when the word becomes flesh. When the statement "by His stripes we are healed" gets to our ears from within, and our body accepts it. Then no disease, even a deadly one, can remain in the body, even when bedsores have formed, even after the surgeon has removed almost everything...The Word of God accomplishes a great and impossible job.

If you trust the Word with every cell in your body, it means that the Word has been revealed to you. Who gave you this revelation? Jesus. The Word of God. It means you let Him fill your mind. (Our mind is a part of our soul.) Your soul transformed according to the word, which rooted itself, germinated and become flesh.

And how does our faith grow?

**_Romans 10:17_
So then faith comes by hearing, and hearing by the word of God.

Faith does not begin with what we can see or feel.

Faith begins with what we cannot see. The moment you make the decision to believe what the Word of God says over what your body feels, then all your spiritual organs respond to your decision and start working according to the word, which you decided to believe.

This was the illustration given by Kenneth Copeland, a famous preacher:

You decide to eat a lemon. You haven't begun eating it yet and only look at it with the intent to eat it. At this moment your mouth fills with saliva. It means that your body responds and reacts to your decision. The same thing happens when you make the decision to believe God about your healing - your whole body responds and the law of the Spirit of life in Jesus Christ is put into motion. You do not see these inner processes, but as long as you believe, it is happening.

**Hebrews 11:1
"Now faith is the substance of things hoped for, the evidence of things not seen."

When our spirit catches the Word, we are able to call those things which do not exist as though they did. The Bible gives many examples to help understand this.

Abraham was old, but believed God's promise about his descendants. He believed at a time when the physical nature of things was in direct opposition of that promise. But he believed God above all hope. He believed God, who gives life to the dead and calls those things which do not exist as though they did. This is what God teaches us. Just as it was in the times of Abraham, when God created something out of that which could not exist, this principle still works for us today. When we trust God's word, our faith is released.

**Romans 4:18-21
"...who, contrary to hope, in hope believed, so that he became the father of many nations, according to what was spoken, "So shall your descendants be." And not being weak in faith, he did not consider his

*own body, already dead (since he was about a hundred years old),
and the deadness of Sarah's womb. He did not waver at the promise
of God through unbelief, but was strengthened in faith, giving glory
to God, and being fully convinced that what He had promised He
was also able to perform."*

Only having received a revelation we can act by faith in spite of what
we see or feel.

To be able to agree to sacrifice Isaac, Abraham must have had the
revelation about God who raises from the dead (Genesis, chapter 22).

The poor widow must have had the revelation about the principles
of God's provision and His laws of multiplication to put in all she had
to live on into the donation box(Luke, chapter 21).

Our faith will be tested. Without it we will not become seasoned, nor
get forged by the strength of Christ. Every product must be tested.

A few years ago my husband and I were invited to work with interior
architects in a lamp factory "Fabbian" in an Italian town Castelfranco
. We were shown all the production processes of their exclusive lamps:
from the concept to the final stage of packaging. We were shown the way
of testing those expensive models: the lamp was placed in a freezer and
held there at a fixed temperature. Then it was placed in a chamber with
a sauna effect where the temperature was constantly rising. This was
how they tested the durability of the lamp. If the materials from which
the lamp is made pass the test, the lamp is put into production. It means
that that particular model gets multiplied. It is distributed all over the
world. "Fabbian" is well known in all developed countries. It does its
job very well and holds its good reputation, for it is the author of every
lamp. Every lamp has a logo of the company as a seal of its creator and
a guarantee that it is made in adherence to the highest world standards
and it will not let anyone down during its service, because the lamp has
passed the test.

Our faith gets stronger as it undergoes tests and pressures.

**Hebrews 10:35-39
Therefore do not cast away your confidence, which has great reward.
For you have need of endurance, so that after you have done the will of
God, you may receive the promise:
"For yet a little while, and He who is coming will come and will not
tarry.
Now the just shall live by faith; but if anyone draws back, My soul has
no pleasure in him."
But we are not of those who draw back to perdition, but of those who
believe to the saving of the soul.

Satan likes when we, having been redeemed from diseases and weaknesses, begin to dwell on our diagnosis. He enjoys it when doubts creep into our soul: did God really say that by His stripes I was healed? Satan does his best to make us believe the diagnosis of this world, his own diagnosis for us, and accept the situation. Or else he wants us to surrender ourselves to doctors and set all our hopes upon their competence.

The acts of holy apostles were described by Luke. He was a doctor, but there is no evidences in the New Testament that Luke healed. Luke describes how people who believed in Jesus healed others, how God healed and raised from the dead by the hand of the Apostle Paul. Is it possible to put handkerchiefs around his body and then send them out as plasters to be used for healing? Paul was looking at those things with the eyes of faith, but not by the physical vision. And God liked that.

If you spend time, every day, reading the Bible which is the Word of Life, your faith will get stronger day by day, while the anxiety and disbelief will be drowned out by the Word of God. Your mind (soul) will be brought to conformity with what the Word says and will reject what the symptoms of the disease say. And now, based on what you learn from the Word of God, you can command these symptoms:

Disease! I am calling you by name...You do not have any authority or power over my body. This body is for the Lord and the Lord for this body. The One who is in me is greater than the one who is in the world. In the name of the Lord I prohibit you, filthy disease, to live in my body. Get out! I believe

God, and not your symptoms. God gave me the power of the Spirit which I use against you. I am in the victory of Jesus Christ! I am healed according to 1 Peter 2:24. This truth is about me. I choose this truth. I say it to you, Satan: "I will not die but live, and proclaim what the Lord has done! In the name of Jesus!"

Ultimately your trust in God will grow beyond average understanding. You will believe the God whom you do not see, more than the symptoms which you feel.

If you pray every day, study the Word of God, put into practice what you have already learned, your faith will grow like the muscles of athletes when they regularly work out. You will become strong and capable to reject everything that does not conform to the Word of God.

To do this you need to know what the Word says about your problem. Search for the verses that speak about healing in the Scripture. During my stay in the hospital's oncological ward my Bible accumulated a multitude of yellow post-its. Yellow is my favorite color. I would read and re-read the Gospel, the Epistles of Paul, Peter, John... When I saw a verse about healing I would mark it with a yellow post-it. Then I would return to that verse several times. I would re-read it. I pondered how it related to me. Of course this took time. But I had lived without God for so long. With all the lack of faith in this world my soul had drawn sustenance from what this cursed world could offer. All of us lived in that way. We believed that what we saw was the only reality. We did not have eyes to see the truth. We looked at the world with the eyes of flesh. Now we are learning to see with the eyes of spirit, by faith. Our future depends on what we see.

God likes it when we are able to step above the heaps of problems while leaning on His Word. We set our hopes upon the Almighty God, our Father. He tells us:"Do not be afraid. Only believe... Do not look at the visible things. They are temporary. Trust Me. I will show you great and impossible things"... He opens our eyes, the eyes of the spirit.

Every time we walk with God through impossible things we become stronger. Our faith in the omnipotence of God becomes stronger. God promises: "When you pass through the waters, I will be with you; and through the rivers, they shall not overflow you. When you walk through the fire, you shall not be burned, nor shall the flame scorch you." (**Isaiah 43:2). He is with us to save us. He is in us, the hope of glory (Colossians 1:27). He arms me with strength (Psalm 18:32). He gives us the instructions when we become weak: "Let the weak say, 'I am strong.'" (Joel 3:10). I am not strong by my weakness. I am strong by the Lord. I draw nourishment from His Word. What a confidence in the Gospel that Paul carried within himself!

**2 Corinthians 12:10
"Therefore I take pleasure in infirmities, in reproaches, in needs, in persecutions, in distresses, for Christ's sake. For when I am weak, then I am strong."

**James 4:7
"Therefore submit to God. Resist the devil and he will flee from you."

When you are obedient to the Word of God and trust God in any situation, in spite of the circumstances of this world, you go against the current. Only live fish can swim against the stream. You go in the direction which is opposite the direction which the whole world goes. The narrow gate... We must withstand! So that we may have life.

From the book "Keeping on doing impossible things" by Oral Roberts (page 269,270)
> *Epigraph: "Having seen the invisible, do the impossible".*
> *"Your faith will be tested. Let me tell you one thing: any dead fish can go downstream. But only live fish will be able to go against the stream. If your faith does not take root in the Son of God deeply enough, if your devotion is not sincere, if your obedience is not enough, you will not withstand trials. You will go down the stream like a dead fish. You will not be able to overcome the circumstances. But it is the victory in this struggle that builds the character of the believer, affirms his testimony and brings joy to the Lord and people. Everyone goes through trials".*

..."The righteous will live by faith". Either you live in faith or die in doubts. Either you stand in faith or fall in compromises. There is no neutral zone. Either you give yourself to faith or to compromise".

When the doctors are powerless before an incurable disease, when you can feel death breathe into your face, when according to all laws of nature your body is no longer fit for normal life, and there is no alternative, except setting all hope upon God and His Word, then the inexplicable power becomes available. This power does not come from the bowels of the earth. It comes from within us.

In order to live by faith you need to be infused with the Word of Life. If you do not choose life, a curse is the only thing that remains. There is no neutral territory! There is no cherry orchard meant for good people! Michael Bulgakov proposed an alternative savior (the book "Master and Margarita"). It is a serious compromise with Satan! Poor Margarita accepted that. We accept Jesus Christ as our Savior. Christians do not fly on a broom. They use a sword, which is the Word of God. This sword separates the emotional things from the spiritual ones.

Hebrews 4:12
"For the word of God is living and powerful, and sharper than any two-edged sword, piercing even to the division of soul and spirit, and of joints and marrow, and is a discerner of the thoughts and intents of the heart."

The Word of God separates sin from righteousness, blessing from curse... You must be on the right side of the separating sword so that you can live.

Galatians 3:13
"Christ has redeemed us from the curse of the law, having become a curse for us for it is written, "Cursed is everyone who hangs on a tree"

Cancer is a diagnosis that falls under the curse of the law. Christ has set us free from that curse. None of the diseases have the right to rule over our bodies. This is the truth. But the truth alone does not automatically negate my diagnosis. It is written that knowing the truth will set you free. Know the truth then, know the Word of living God. It will set you free from any curse of this world, including diseases. The faith was given to us. We need to put it to use.

**_Romans 10:17_
"So then faith comes by hearing, and hearing by the word of God."

Do not be distracted from the Scriptures! Move away from the fuss! When cancer is hard at work 24 hours a day, it is not enough to spend 10 minutes a day reading God's word. It is not enough! Is it really easier to let the surgeons remove everything from our body than abide in the Word?

Paul was an average man of small stature who suffered a lot and whose body was crippled with stones and multiple beatings. But he was a man of great faith. He was the one who hell knew personally. When Paul appeared diseases took a step back, just as they stepped away in the presence of Jesus. He was not alone when he walked around and evangelized. The power of the Almighty God, which raised Christ from the dead, was with him. The same power raised Paul from the dead when he was beaten with stones. Paul used the same power to raise people from the dead. That power was the power of the Holy Spirit. The Holy Spirit is ready to act today. But He needs our faith. The power of the Spirit is displayed in the power of the word that is spoken with faith. When we develop and build up our faith we can achieve impossible things. And our Heavenly Father rejoices at our achievements of faith.

"There is something in trusting God, that induces God to make the round of a million people to reach you" (Smith Wigglesworth)

Pray with me.
Father! I thank You for the faith through which I can reach all the promises that You have given me. Thank You for the word about my healing and for my belief in it. I can live not by what I see but what I believe in. I thank You!

I believe that the power of Your Word accomplishes the work of healing. You sent Your Word and healed me. I believe in it and insist that I am healed from head to toe. I believe, my Lord, that there is no disease which You did not take up onto the cross on Calvary. I believe that I am free from any weakness or disease, because You have redeemed me. And this is forever. That is why I resist any disorder in my body with strong faith. By faith I say: I am redeemed. I am healed. I am not in want of anything. There is nothing broken or missing in my body. This is the truth about me.

I thank You for giving me life and health! I am a new creature in Jesus Christ. For as long as I believe in it, it is true.

Amen!

Chapter 7

Life and death are in the power of the tongue

**Proverbs 18:21*
"Death and life are in the power of the tongue, and those who love it will eat its fruit."

Our words can carry information and as a consequence they are the carriers of faith or fear, blessing or curse, life or death... We have the power to make changes in our life.

If we believe in the Bible, then we know that in the beginning was the Word, and without Him nothing was made...

**John 1:1-4*
1. "In the beginning was the Word, and the Word was with God, and the Word was God.
2. He was in the beginning with God.
3. All things were made through Him, and without Him nothing was made that was made.

4. In Him was life, and the life was the light of men".

In order for something to be, a word must be released. And this word will spring into life. If you speak a negative word, that word will proceed to live and cause a negative influence. If instead you speak words of life (the Bible is called the Book of life), these words will carry life-giving strength, the strength to live. If you let yourself believe what you say, the words you speak - materialize.

When a problem comes into your home, do not rush to vocalize the situation. Do not confirm it with a word, because by doing so you will be giving the problem a life force. Do not call these things by their names. All visible things are temporary. Call them just like God calls them. Speak the words of victory into your life.

There are some spiritual principles which allow us to turn around any undesirable circumstance. God teaches us to say what He says, not what the circumstances say, about ourselves.

**Joel 3:10
"...Let the weak say, 'I am strong.'"

When you are in need or loss, confess by faith: "And my God shall supply all your need according to His riches in glory by Christ Jesus." (Philippians 4:19)

If you are sick, confess by faith: "... by whose stripes you were healed. "(1Peter 2:24)

And the Lord, as the High Priest of our confession, fulfills every pronounced word of faith.

**Numbers 14:28
"Say to them, 'As I live,' says the LORD, 'just as you have spoken in My hearing, so I will do to you..."

If you say by faith: "I am healed" at the moment when your body still displays all symptoms of a bad flu, you will not be lying. It means that you agree with the word that says you are healed. The healing belongs to you regardless of what your body tells you about it.

**_Mark 11:23_
"For assuredly, I say to you, whoever says to this mountain, 'Be re-moved and be cast into the sea,' and does not doubt in his heart, but believes that those things he says will be done, he will have whatever he says."

It is written here that WE ourselves must command this mountain. We must do as God does. How? God does not wait for the circumstances to change before He speaks about them. God's word makes them change. We can do the same if we bring our words to conformity with His words and speak by faith. Even if it seems that the circumstances do not change at once, do not vocalize that fact. You do not know the real state of the situation in the invisible spiritual world. All visible things are temporary. The fact is that, if the Word of God says that everything will be according to your words (if you do not doubt it), then so it will be. Perhaps it will not be evident in the visible world right away, but in the invisible world it will be as you have said. Words carry definite information. Jesus commanded the fig tree to dry up and did not check the condition of the tree after that (Mark 11:14). He spoke the words and knew that it was done and that it would be as He said. The next morning everyone saw that for themselves and was convinced. The word materialized.

It was clear enough for me what the consequences of chemotherapy were like. For a long time I was surrounded by women who either had gone through the procedures already or were going through them at the same time as I. One of these side-effects was obvious - alopecia (hair loss). When a person feels practically dead, appearance becomes irrelevant. But I can tell you that it mattered to me. I was not preparing myself for death. Nor did I behave as a person who was clinging to life. I simply continued to live. At the time I was still teaching. I thought to myself: "To look this way even if you are a teacher of interior design will be too much of a creative statement". But how to stop the hair loss? How could I resist? When I washed my hair the bathtub would be filled with it. Every time I ran my fingers through my hair I would be left holding a bunch in my hand.

At that time I was constantly reading the Bible. I understood that the answer was there. At one point the words which I had read so many times and I knew by heart, suddenly "sprung up" before my eyes in a whole new light.

**_Luke 12:7_
"But the very hairs of your head are all numbered. Do not fear therefore; you are of more value than many sparrows."

**_Luke 21:18_
"But not a hair of your head shall be lost."

Then I realized that God takes responsibility for His every word. He answers for the fact that not a hair from my head shall be lost. I am worthy in His eyes, otherwise He would not have paid such a high price for my salvation, the price of His Blood.

I did not even ask in my prayer to save my hair. I just called into being the non-existent things in the face of the existent hair loss: "Not a hair of my head will be lost. For the very hairs of my head are all numbered". The hair kept on falling, but I kept standing on the word: "Not a hair of my head will be lost". And you know what? I did not become bald. I did not buy a wig. And today the hair on my head is perfectly all right.

During the disease all my creative activity stopped.

Could I possibly be of interest to those who were working under my supervision in 2005, when I was diagnosed with cancer and nothing spoken in favor of my future life, let alone career? There was no one left beside me, except God and my family. My business stopped functioning. People who seek advice must be confident in the strength of their adviser. The customers disappeared. What client would want to invest into a nearly dead person? Completing a project takes much devoted time. I did not have any. I was dying. No amount of money could solve that problem. The fact that I am alive now is not to the credit of the doctors. It was not by the help of people whose houses I had decorated. My customers were wealthy enough and there was no financial crisis at the time. None thought to ask: "Can I do something for you?" My answer would, anyway, be: "No". It was impossible for a man. Only God could do that. If I am an architect, an author of a particular project, I would know how to correct this project. God is my Author. He raised me from the dead as soon as I drew nearer to Him. (This is my recommendation. The choice is always your own to make).

I did not just want to survive then, I wanted to survive for the purpose of doing good work. It was a difficult time for me. In the morning my body went through exhausting procedures of traditional medicine and in the evening I taught a class. I continued to teach the interior design course. Every time I entered the lecture room, after overcoming a torturous climb of the old high stairwell to get to the fourth floor (How I hated those stairs and my inability to overcome the last few), I would make a statement: "My friends! I do not know if I will be here for the next lecture. Whether I will be at all..." Afterwards I would go home, shaking in pain on an overcrowded bus and not always having a seat...

I tell you today that with the words: "Will I still be?", "Can I?", "Do I want?"...I may as well walk myself to my own funeral service, because if I am in a state of "I do not know", "I am not sure", "I doubt", Satan will very quickly figure out what to do with it. All he needs is our confession that will be in accordance with the misery we see and feel.

It was the wrong confession of my lips. By confessing factual things, I was confirming the existing situation. The situation did not need a confirmation, it needed to be radically changed! I no longer act this way. Instead, I say to the Lord: "He is my refuge and my fortress; my God, in Him I will trust."(**Psalm 91:2)

James 3:11
"Does a spring send forth fresh water and bitter from the same opening?"

If you made the decision to watch your tongue, not to speak any words of defeat, but to confess only what the Word of God says..., be constant in it. If in the morning you take a stand in prayer, to resist the symptoms of arthritis and repeat with boldness:"No harm will befall me! No weapon forged against me will prevail! The Lord protects all my bones, not one of them will be broken...", then you should not later in the day tell everyone on the phone that your bones cannot stand the changing temperature and this condition usually takes so many days before you feel better, and your tongue is tired from proclaiming the protection of the Blood of Jesus on your bones so many times... Do not be like this! Do not change so quickly! Do not destroy the work you did in prayer that morning. Give the seed of the word a chance to grow. For there is nothing hidden that will not be disclosed. Remain constant. Only the words of victory, not of defeat, must be heard in your house. It must become your way of life. You will definitely see the result of your mouth's confession, but only if do not nullify it with the words of doubt, disbelief and anxiety.

****1Peter 3:10*
"For he who would love life and see good days, let him refrain his tongue from evil, and his lips from speaking deceit."

Do you love life? Do you want to see many good days of it? Put some effort into training your tongue. Learn to control your language. Do not speak idle useless words that will occupy valuable space in your mind which should instead be filled with life-giving truth. The truth is: "By the stripes of Jesus you are healed".

From the book "Pursuit of His Presence" by Kenneth and Gloria Copeland (January the 20th)
Own Your Healing
...If you need healing today, you must capture the land of healing. You must stand on the Word of God and say: "The healing belongs to me. The devil will not steal it from me. Nobody will dissuade me from it. It is mine. Today, right now, I receive my healing!"

Having said this, never say anything to the contrary. Do not be led by time, symptoms or something else. Hold your ground. Continue to take God's medicine, His Word, every day, and you will become more and more healthy.

Pray with me.

Dear Lord! I sincerely repent now of every idle word which came out of my mouth but did not correspond with Your truth. Forgive me for every idle word. Forgive me for the words of irritation and accusation... I repent! I denounce every rotten word. I do not want such words to stand in the way of my healing.

I make the decision to speak into my life only the words of victory, the words which correspond with what the Word of God says about me. I speak into my life: "Lord Who forgives all my iniquities, Who heals all my diseases, Who redeems my life from destruction, Who crowns me with lovingkindness and tender mercies, Who satisfies my mouth with good things, so that my youth is renewed like the eagle's.(**Psalm 103:3-5).

Help me, Lord, to become a spring which sends forth life and joy, healing and peace, power and wisdom... Teach me to control my emotions and rule my tongue according to Your words: "...let every man be swift to hear, slow to speak, slow to wrath..." (**James 1:19).

Help me, Lord, to be such a person. Amen!

Chapter 8

You shall receive power when the Ḣoly Spirit has come upon you

Acts 1:4,5,8,9
4. "And being assembled together with them, He commanded them not to depart from Jerusalem, but to wait for the Promise of the Father, "which," He said, "you have heard from Me;
5. for John truly baptized with water, but you shall be baptized with the Holy Spirit not many days from now."
8. But you shall receive power when the Holy Spirit has come upon you; and you shall be witnesses to Me in Jerusalem, and in all Judea and Samaria, and to the end of the earth."
9. Now when He had spoken these things, while they watched, He was taken up, and a cloud received Him out of their sight."

In ten days the Holy Spirit came upon them. It happened in Jerusalem on the Day of the Pentecost in the room filled with 120 people.

Acts 2:1-4
1. "When the Day of Pentecost had fully come, they were all with one accord[a] in one place.

2. And suddenly there came a sound from heaven, as of a rushing mighty wind, and it filled the whole house where they were sitting.
3. Then there appeared to them divided tongues, as of fire, and one sat upon each of them.
4. And they were all filled with the Holy Spirit and began to speak with other tongues, as the Spirit gave them utterance. "

The Holy Spirit came upon everyone who was born again. The whole room was illuminated with fire. They were not tiny flames on their heads. Everyone who followed Christ became enveloped in the flames of the Holy Spirit. And they began to speak with other tongues, as the Spirit gave them utterance: sha-da-rıka-tariba-sadara...It was the only physical manifestation of the Spirit in them – they spoke with other tongues (see Exodus 3:2). Every one became a torch of fire that would not burn out. They received the power, when the Holy Spirit came upon them. The power! It was the same power with which David went against Goliaph. The same power that divided the waters of the Sea of Reeds allowing the people of Israel cross the sea on dry land. This very power made the sun stand still until Joshua achieved victory and made the shadow cast by the sun go ten steps back as a sign of healing for king Hezekiah. This power gave birth to Jesus and later raised Him from the dead. This is His power. We have the same power within. Satan cannot conquer us, because God is with us. The One Who is in us is greater than the one who is in the world. Jesus says that anything is possible for him who believes (Mark 9:23), who believes the One Who is Almighty.

Believing in the existence of God is not enough to overcome an incurable disease. It is not enough to believe that God heals. It is essential that the power of God is living and active in the life of a believer, governing him and protecting him from destruction. The more Holy Spirit governs the life of a believer the more God's power works in his life. Without Him we are helpless in this world.

Being born again and being baptized with the Holy Spirit are not the same thing. We repent of our sins and give our life to Jesus – He cleanses us of sins, diseases and filth of this world. He paid for us with His Blood 2000 years ago, He paid for our sins and won us for the Kingdom of God and the eternal life. We become new creatures in Christ Jesus. He comes into our life as the Lord. Then He gives us the power. He clothes us in His Spirit. We cannot receive this power if we are not a new creature. No mortal person can experience the real presence of God and stay alive. But after we are born again, our nature changes. God's own nature begins to work within us and we become capable of living in His power (as Adam did long time ago). In the spiritual world the power of the Holy Spirit is like a fire.

John the Baptist was born to prepare the world for the baptism of the Holy Spirit. Having been baptized with water (repentance), having been cleansed of sins, people could be baptized with the Spirit and accept His power.

>### ****Luke 3:16**
> *John answered, saying to all, "I indeed baptize you with water; but One mightier than I is coming, whose sandal strap I am not worthy to loose. He will baptize you with the Holy Spirit and fire.*

>### ****Acts 19:1-7**
> *1. And it happened, while Apollos was at Corinth, that Paul, having passed through the upper regions, came to Ephesus. And finding some disciples*
> *2. he said to them, "Did you receive the Holy Spirit when you believed?" So they said to him, "We have not so much as heard whether there is a Holy Spirit."*
> *3. And he said to them, "Into what then were you baptized?"*
> *So they said, "Into John's baptism."*
> *4. Then Paul said, "John indeed baptized with a baptism of repentance, saying to the people that they should believe on Him who would come after him, that is, on Christ Jesus."*
> *5. When they heard this, they were baptized in the name of the Lord Jesus.*
> *6. And when Paul had laid hands on them, the Holy Spirit came upon them, and they spoke with tongues and prophesied.*
> *7. Now the men were about twelve in all.*

"They spoke with tongues..." The tongues which are different from those we know and hear. The Holy Spirit within us creates His supernatural language. In that way He gives revelation, vision and prophecy to our mind, strengthens our faith, teaches us, reveals the Word to us so that we could learn about Lord Jesus. He gives us the anointing and all necessary spiritual equipment. Thus, with His power, we receive everything that God considers to be necessary for us.

When you pray in tongues, you often do not understand what you pray about unless God has given you the gift of interpreting tongues. But this kind of prayer is absolutely perfect and in its divine form it gets to the right destination. This prayer is always heard, because it is made by the Holy Spirit within our spirit. He appeals on our behalf! He knows why we are weak. He knows why we cannot accept healing, He knows all of our needs and cares for us. He knows everything and we know nothing. He knows how we should pray when we do not. He is always ready to pray through us about everything we care for. He does need to pray for Himself, because all is well with Him. He prays for us! He has a desire to teach us the truth that can make us free.

**_John 8:32_
"And you shall know the truth, and the truth shall make you free."

The Holy Spirit reveals God's secrets to us. We become transformed by the power of His word which He imparts unto us through His supernatural language. The answer about our healing, freeing our children from addictions, getting out of debt may be contained in a few words incomprehensible our mind... No one knows our calling better than the Holy Spirit. Every time you pray in tongues you are praying in agreement with God's will.

**_Romans 8:26_
"Likewise the Spirit also helps in our weaknesses. For we do not know what we should pray for as we ought, but the Spirit Himself makes intercession for us with groans which cannot be uttered."

You should not be afraid to speak in this incomprehensible language, regardless what tradition and religion have to say. Look for the answer in the Word of God. You cannot read the Bible while skipping lines. The Apostle Paul prayed in tongues more than anyone else. He wrote more epistles of the New Testament than the other apostles. However, it was not him, but the grace of God made that possible.

> ****1Corinphians 14:18**
> *"I thank my God I speak with tongues more than you all..."*

He recommends us:

> *"I wish you all spoke with tongues..." (**1Corinphians 14:5)*

Apostle Paul went through all sorts of trials in his life. His life in Christ was one heroic act of faith. He learned to live and to survive in any conditions and circumstances of this world. Not everyone could survive in such conditions. Paul was and he is (because those in God never die) the man of God. It means that his life and his works were supernaturally unusual in God's way. Even if it seemed that he did not have anything, Paul knew that he had everything. He knew it from the Holy Spirit Who Himself had taught him. Paul knew that Jesus has given him the power over demons, weakness and diseases. And hell itself was aware of this. Demons would say: "I know Jesus, I know Paul...", because Paul applied the power he received from the Lord. And demons obeyed him. Paul walked in the power of the Holy Spirit.

> ****Acts 19:11-16**
> *"Now God worked unusual miracles by the hands of Paul, so that even handkerchiefs or aprons were brought from his body to the sick, and the diseases left them and the evil spirits went out of them. Then some of the itinerant Jewish exorcists took it upon themselves to call the name of the Lord Jesus over those who had evil spirits, saying, "We exorcise you by the Jesus whom Paul preaches." Also there were seven sons of Sceva, a Jewish chief priest, who did so.*
> *And the evil spirit answered and said, "Jesus I know, and Paul I know; but who are you?"*
> *Then the man in whom the evil spirit was leaped on them, overpowered[b] them, and prevailed against them,[c] so that they fled out of that house naked and wounded.*

Paul's life was a test of great faith. Paul had the ability to face death without fear. And when death came to him at one point, Paul simply shook it off and came back into the town where he was stoned and proceeded to preach. He knew with certainty that death did not have power over him. Grace has done a great work on him. It is a fact. The same grace is within us. Paul wrote:

**2Corinphians 13:14
14 The grace of the Lord Jesus Christ, and the love of God, and the communion of the Holy Spirit be with you all. Amen.

It says: "the communion of the Holy Spirit". The Holy Spirit desires to communicate with us. We should also desire it. No one else can truly reveal the Word of God to us. (The Bible was written by people inspired by the Holy Spirit. No one else can protect and heal us. All miracles of healing and deliverance happen on earth by the Holy Spirit – the third person of the Holy Trinity. He is God Who is always with us on earth. He is the Promise, the Gift, the Seal, the Guarantee of our salvation...

Every one of us should have this gift so that we could learn to give free reign to the power of the Holy Spirit, Who is within us. He desperately desires to lead us in prayer hour after hour, revealing our secrets to God and God's secrets to us. The prayer in tongues always bears good fruit. If we spend time every day, praying in tongues, our life becomes transformed- spirit, body and soul. We transform according to the truth about us. The truth is that we have already been healed 2000 years ago. Now our transformation is required. And this is the work of the Holy Spirit in us. Our job is to find the time for it. To pray in tongues for 10 minutes a day is very little! Cancer works around the clock in destroying a person's body! The devil works on his plan of your destruction 24 hours a day, 7 days a week. But we have grace – to be in the presence and under the protection of the Holy Spirit all the time. We need to be charged from the Holy Spirit and the Word of life every day of the week.

**Jude 1:20,21
"But you, beloved, building yourselves up on your most holy faith, praying in the Holy Spirit, keep yourselves in the love of God, looking for the mercy of our Lord Jesus Christ unto eternal life."

When I talk to people who are sick but believe in the divine healing, I usually ask them one question: "Are you baptized In the Holy Spirit?" The same question Paul asked his disciples in Ephes.

**Acts 19:1-7
"And it happened, while Apollos was at Corinth, that Paul, having passed through the upper regions, came to Ephesus. And finding some disciples he said to them, "Did you receive the Holy Spirit when you believed?"
So they said to him, "We have not so much as heard whether there is a Holy Spirit."
And he said to them, "Into what then were you baptized?"
So they said, "Into John's baptism." Then Paul said, "John indeed baptized with a baptism of repentance, saying to the people that they should believe on Him who would come after him, that is, on Christ Jesus."

When they heard this, they were baptized in the name of the Lord Jesus. And when Paul had laid hands on them, the Holy Spirit came upon them, and they spoke with tongues and prophesied. Now the men were about twelve in all."

When we are baptized in the Holy Spirit, He begins to lead us through life and brings us up in the spirit of faith. I did not have my own strength or willpower to withstand cancer or alcoholism. He has all the power. He gives it to us. We always have protection. God said: "I will never leave you nor forsake you". The Holy Spirit is always with us to the very end of the age. He is with us, to lead us on this earth, until the end filling us with His power, teaching us to withstand any disease. He wishes to bring us to the Heavenly Father as co-heirs with Jesus Christ, raised up in faith and having received all His promises.

Without Him we will be lost and hardly be victorious. Let the Holy Spirit make you strong believers so that you could take possession of your healing in strong faith, as well as salvation and deliverance of your children and all the other promises that the Heavenly Father has prepared for you. One of the most important keys to a powerful faith, that which can exorcise the devil and the diseases he brings, is a prayer in tongues.

> *From the book "Power born of the Spirit"("The Walk of the Spirit – the walk of Power")* by Dave Roberson (page 205, 228)..
>
> *A limited way of thinking is the only barrier between us and every possible miracle. With such mentality faith is rendered helpless, or to be more precise, there can be no faith at all. Such mentality is followed by unfulfilled hopes, fears and suffering.*
>
> *The Holy Spirit will surely replace this turmoil with a hope so strong that faith will make it into reality. But we ought to be obedient to His guidance when He begins to uproot this wrong mentality. Otherwise we will remain prisoners of this invisible jail until the end of our lives.*
>
> *I think there is nothing to add, except prayer.*

Pray with me.

Dear Father! I ask You to fill me with the Holy Spirit! Fill me with the power of Your Spirit, so that I could resist all weakness, disease and any other curse of this world. According to Luke 11:13, I believe that You give the Holy Spirit to those who ask You.

In faith, I receive the baptism in the Holy Spirit. I believe that I will speak tongues as You, Holy Spirit, enable me. I will not be the same. In faith I receive the power with which I will be able to withstand any work of the devil in my life and also to preach good news to the poor, to bind up the brokenhearted, give sight to the blind, and proclaim freedom and the release from darkness for the captives... in the name of Jesus Christ.

In faith I say: the Spirit of the Sovereign Lord is upon me! He has anointed me!

Amen!

Chapter 9

Behold, I give you the authority

**_Luke 10:19_
Behold, I give you the authority to trample on serpents and scorpions,
and over all the power of the enemy, and nothing shall by any means
hurt you.

According to God's will we are the bearers of His power, His authority and His armor which He has given us so that we could resist any enemy on this earth. If we have an understanding this authority we will not set our hopes upon ourselves. We will rely on the power of God.

In three of the Gospels (Matthew, Mark and Luke) there is a description of one particular day, when Jesus gave His disciples power and authority and commanded to exorcise demons and heal the sick.

In chapter 9 of the Gospel of Matthew — Jesus, as a teacher, displayed the manifestation of His authority and the release of miracles by the power of the Holy Spirit. One by one, He performed miracles that defied comprehension: He raised a paralyzed boy onto his feet, healed a woman from a 12-year bleeding problem, raised a girl from the dead, gave sight to the blind, and exorcised the demons from the mute possessed man, after which the latter began to speak. These are the recorded miracles. Besides that, Jesus continued to teach in synagogues and preach the Gospel of the Kingdom and heal every weakness and disease in the people who followed Him in crowds. Every weakness and disease!

And in chapter 10 of the Gospel by Matthew the disciples are given the authority by Jesus equipping them to do the same things as Jesus did:

**<u>*Matthew 10:7,8*</u>
And as you go, preach, saying, 'The kingdom of heaven is at hand.' Heal the sick, cleanse the lepers, raise the dead, cast out demons. Freely you have received, freely give.

Please note that healing, cleansing, and raising from the dead are separated by commas, which means that they are equally possible for God to accomplish. God is just as powerful to raise from the dead as He is to heal. He is powerful with the power of His Spirit. Now the Spirit of the Lord God is upon us. And these signs will follow those who believe.

**<u>*Mark 16:17,18,20*</u>
17. And these signs will follow those who believe: In My name they will cast out demons; they will speak with new tongues;
18. they will take up serpents; and if they drink anything deadly, it will by no means hurt them; they will lay hands on the sick, and they will recover."
20. And they went out and preached everywhere, the Lord working with them and confirming the word through the accompanying signs. Amen.

Jesus gave us the same commission as He received from His Father. This we read in the book of the prophet Isaiah:

**<u>*Isaiah 61:1-3*</u>
1. "The Spirit of the Lord GOD is upon Me, Because the LORD has anointed Me To preach good tidings to the poor; He has sent Me to heal the brokenhearted, To proclaim liberty to the captives, And the opening of the prison to those who are bound;

2. To proclaim the acceptable year of the LORD, And the day of vengeance of our God; To comfort all who mourn,
3. To console those who mourn in Zion, To give them beauty for ashes, aw The garment of praise for the spirit of heaviness; That they may be called trees of righteousness, The planting of the LORD, that He may be glorified."

This commission forestalled that which would happen after Jesus accomplished His victory on Calvary and gave His followers an incomparable gift of the baptism in the Holy Spirit. All the miracles that Jesus performed on earth were not by the means of God ministering to the people from Heaven, but by a man of flesh-Jesus, Who operated in the gifts of the Holy Spirit while living on Earth. The same manifestation of spiritual gifts is available to people today. Do you believe in what Jesus says?

**John 14:12
"Most assuredly, I say to you, he who believes in Me, the works that I do he will do also; and greater works than these he will do, because I go to My Father.

You may feel that the Lord did not provide you with the same power, and that the gifts of the Holy Spirit are not for you. But as long as you are in this world you will have to learn how to act as people who have power and to do the works the Lord requires. Otherwise you will perish sooner or later, because the power of sin, disease and epidemics is constantly attacking. If you refuse to use this power and authority (to fight), you will be drowned out by with relentless, filthy flows of this world. Although, we are in the world, we are not of this world. Satan rules many things but he does not control me. He does not rule the Church. He does not rule us. We must to rule him. We have the authority over him. Jesus said:

**Luke 10:19
Behold, I give you the authority to trample on serpents and scorpions, and over all the power of the enemy, and nothing shall by any means hurt you.

All the authority given by Jesus must be manifested through the Church, that is – through us, because Jesus Himself is no longer present here in His physical body. He lives within us by the Holy Spirit.

**Matthew 28:18-20
And Jesus came and spoke to them, saying, "All authority has been given to Me in heaven and on earth. Go therefore and make disciples of all the nations, baptizing them in the name of the Father and of the Son and of the Holy Spirit, teaching them to observe all things that I have commanded you; and lo, I am with you always, even to the end of the age." Amen.

We have the authority whether we realize it or not.

Apostle Paul's epistle to the Ephesians speaks in detail about the authority of the believer. At the end of chapters 1 and 3 there are prayers anointed by the Spirit. These prayers concern us just as much as they concerned the believers in Ephes, because Paul was led by the Holy Spirit to write them.

**Ephesians 1:16-23
16. do not cease to give thanks for you, making mention of you in my prayers:
17. that the God of our Lord Jesus Christ, the Father of glory, may give to you the spirit of wisdom and revelation in the knowledge of Him,
18. the eyes of your understanding[c] being enlightened; that you may know what is the hope of His calling, what are the riches of the glory of His inheritance in the saints,
19. and what is the exceeding greatness of His power toward us who believe, according to the working of His mighty power
20. which He worked in Christ when He raised Him from the dead and seated Him at His right hand in the heavenly places,
21. far above all principality and power and might and dominion, and every name that is named, not only in this age but also in that which is to come.
22. And He put all things under His feet, and gave Him to be head over all things to the church,
23. which is His body, the fullness of Him who fills all in all.

**Ephesians 3:14-19
14. For this reason I bow my knees to the Father of our Lord Jesus Christ,
15. from whom the whole family in heaven and earth is named,
16. that He would grant you, according to the riches of His glory, to be strengthened with might through His Spirit in the inner man,
17. that Christ may dwell in your hearts through faith; that you, being rooted and grounded in love,
18. may be able to comprehend with all the saints what is the width and length and depth and height
19. to know the love of Christ which passes knowledge; that you may be filled with all the fullness of God.

From the book of Kenneth E. Hagin "The Believer's Authority"
We need to have this spirit of wisdom and revelation about Christ and His Word if we want to grow. We will not receive it through our mind. It must be opened to us by the Holy Spirit...

As a result of my researches I came to the conclusion that we as Church have such authority on the earth which we have not realized yet, the authority which we do not use... Only few of us have touched the edge of this authority, but before Jesus comes back there will be a whole group of people who will use their authority. They will know what belongs to them by right and they will accomplish the work which God has provided for them.

Why do people lose the healing they received during a church service where the gifts of the Spirit were at work? Because their faith lacks foundation, and the devil comes again with false symptoms and make them hostage to disease. Why do they lose their healing? Because they do not know their own authority. They do not know how to hold on to it. We defeat the devil when we are rooted in the foundation of the Word of God, and we live and act by this word. The Word of God teaches us how resist devil and his diseases.

**1Peter 5:9
Resist him, steadfast in the faith...

The level of our faith is directly proportional to how deep the Word of God is in our heart, and whether this word is real to us and whether we stand on it every day.

We need to learn how to take on this authority so that we could confirm the victory of Christ. And we need to know more about it.

From the book of Makhesh Chavda "Hidden power of prayer and fast" (page 61)

Where is the army?

The rangers of Texas who maintained law and order in the Old West once stopped respecting the law. The sheriff of the town of Texas sent an express telegram to the high command of the rangers: "Send the army! The people are turning into rabble. They are rebelling, and this anarchy can destroy us!" Very soon he received a laconic answer: "Expect the 4 o'clock train". Next morning the anxious sheriff and an even more anxious major were standing on the platform waiting for the train. Very soon they saw one solitary ranger came out of the coach, holding his Winchester. Astonished they both turned their eyes from the ranger to the departing train. When the train vanished from sight they grew pale. They came up to the ranger and asked him with anxiety: "Where is the army?" The ranger looked them in the face and said gravely: "One mutiny — one ranger".

He was all they needed, because the ranger knew who he was, whom he presented and he realized full measure of his authority as a representative of the law.

My words to you are very simple: "God prepared for you a personal mutiny to deal with, Ranger. Your task is to feel what God feels to the surrounding world and do something after that. According to God's will you are a bearer of His power. His authority. His arms...

From the book of Kenneth and Gloria Copeland "Pursuit of His Presence" (January the 18th)

God gave you the authority in your life just as He gave the authority to Adam in Eden. You have the authority over your family and your

*house. If you do not make your authority known, the devil will come
and capture your garden just as he captured Eden, Adam's garden.*

*When both Kenneth and I were born again we did not understand
that. We continued to encounter and suffer from the same problems as
when we were in the world.*

*Of course we knew that God performs miracles. Kenneth witnessed
them himself when he was working as a pilot, flying with Oral Roberts
to his healing services. During these services Kenneth's job was to
prepare the disabled people seated in the tent for Oral Roberts who
ministered to them.*

*The tent for the disabled was a place for people who were so ill that
they could not participate in the general service. Most of them were in
wheelchairs or in the last stages of incurable disease.*

*But when brother Roberts I would lay his hands upon them,
Kenneth saw amazing miracles take place. One woman spit out the
cancer tumour right onto the floor. A paralyzed girl who was strapped to
a special stretcher just jumped out of that stretcher and ran, completely
healed, after brother Roberts had touched her.*

*Kenneth saw those miracles with his own eyes. But you know
something? They did not do anything for our family. Our life changed
only after we heard that Jesus has taken our diseases and carried our
weaknesses.*

*When we saw in the Word of God that we had the authority over
our diseases and began proclaiming that truth, freedom came into our
life. When we realized that we were not the sick trying to be healed,
but it was the devil who tried to steal our health, we began to use our
authority and say: "Devil, get out of here!" And he fled, taking his
diseases with him.*

*Surely it is wonderful to see how God performs His miracles. But
you will not be able to live by miracles day by day. Your life will
change when you take the authority which belongs to you according
to the Word of God and release this authority with your mouth. If
you do it, you will be able to hold him under your feet where he is
supposed to be.*

If you need healing today, you must capture it. You must stand on the Word of God and say:

In the name of Jesus! The healing belongs to me. The devil will not steal it from me. It is mine. God gave me the authority over demons, diseases and death. That is why I take the authority over any situation which does not conform to the Word of God about me.

Listen to me, Satan! In the name of Jesus Christ of Nazareth I bind you and all the symptoms of disease in my life, for I have the authority to trample over all the power of the enemy. Nothing will harm me. I resist you with strong faith. My faith is Jesus Who redeemed me from the curse of the law with His blood and won a victory over cancer, death, AIDS, and hell... I am in Him. I am in His victory. Every cell of my body, soul and spirit live according to the law of spirit of life in Jesus Christ. In Him I have integrity. I have divine health as a new person who has been healed by His wounds. I proclaim my body healed and functional, according to the law of spirit of life. I proclaim my children saved, taught by the Lord. I say by faith that my house and I will serve the Lord. I insist that all my needs are supplied by Jesus Christ. I am not in want. I agree with the Word of God in all areas of my life! Satan, I proclaim you helpless and powerless, for Jesus deprived you of power and authority. You are harmless. I believe it. No weapon forged against me will prevail.

I thank my God who has given such authority to the man.
Amen!

Chapter 10

Sin no more, lest a worse thing come upon you

**_John 5:1-14_
1. After this there was a feast of the Jews, and Jesus went up to Jerusalem.
2. Now there is in Jerusalem by the Sheep Gate a pool, which is called in Hebrew, Bethesda,[a] having five porches.
3. In these lay a great multitude of sick people, blind, lame, paralyzed, waiting for the moving of the water.
4. For an angel went down at a certain time into the pool and stirred up the water; then whoever stepped in first, after the stirring of the water, was made well of whatever disease he had.[b]
5. Now a certain man was there who had an infirmity thirty-eight years.
6. When Jesus saw him lying there, and knew that he already had been in that condition a long time, He said to him, "Do you want to be made well?"
7. The sick man answered Him, "Sir, I have no man to put me into the pool when the water is stirred up; but while I am coming, another steps down before me."

8. Jesus said to him, "Rise, take up your bed and walk."
9. And immediately the man was made well, took up his bed, and walked. And that day was the Sabbath.
10. The Jews therefore said to him who was cured, "It is the Sabbath; it is not lawful for you to carry your bed."
11. He answered them, "He who made me well said to me, 'Take up your bed and walk.'"
12. Then they asked him, "Who is the Man who said to you, 'Take up your bed and walk'?"
13. But the one who was healed did not know who it was, for Jesus had withdrawn, a multitude being in that place.
14. Afterward Jesus found him in the temple, and said to him, "See, you have been made well. Sin no more, lest a worse thing come upon you."

That "worse thing" can mean diseases and in the absolute worst case it can mean death (there is nothing worse).

**_Romans 6:23_
23. For the wages of sin is death, but the gift of God is eternal life in Christ Jesus our Lord.

The man in Bethesda was made well — his flesh which had been sick for 38 years was healed. The flesh suffers as man sins. Sin and diseases walk hand in hand. There is a direct connection: from sin -to disease, -to death. We sin because our flesh provokes us. Then the very same flesh suffers from diseases. Flesh and spirit are in conflict with one another (when the spirit is renewed and passes from death to life, it means the man is born again). If a man is not connected to life, his spirit is dead, so it does not react to the destruction of its body.

"Go an sin no more!" I first heard this phrase in 1999, when, being highly intoxicated, I ran into my pastor. She trusted in God. And God knew her. She prayed for me and received my deliverance from God, for me. My mind was not renewed, my flesh was in conflict with the spirit of my pastor. Without having trust in God I sinned again and, as it is written, "a worse thing came upon me". Having sinned I opened the door for Satan and he burst into my life to strike at that which was dearest to me. My son was brought from school in a state of shock – his leg was completely encased in a plaster cast. He slipped and fell on a completely even surface in the school gym, fracturing hid leg in two places. I realized that it was my fault! I aided Satan's purpose. My most beloved person on the earth was suffering because of me! I was overwhelmed with guilt. My heart was breaking and my guilt caused me more suffering than the worst of hangovers. Contrite in spirit I fell down before God... That day I died for sin. God drew me close to Him. He healed my son. Not at once. That time I could only be in two places: at my son's bedside and at church. God was healing my sick soul and brought up my faith in His Word. He took my home under His cover and blocked the way of the destroying angel.

**Numbers 12.
I believe that Miriam was stricken by leprosy in a split moment. I also believe that in seven days she was healed, after Moses' heartfelt prayer to God on her behalf. The cause of Miriam's leprosy was a sin against a man and against God.

There is one more story that is mentioned in three different books of the Bible (2 Chronicles 32:24-26; Isaiah 38:9-12; 2 Kings 20:1-5). It is written in the Scriptures that behind any disease there is a reason. Hezekiah was under the law of sin and that is why he died as a consequence of his disease. God had no plan to kill Hezekiah and did not send the disease upon him. It was a consequence of his own sin.

**1John 3:14
We know that we have passed from death to life...

**John 3:16
For God so loved the world that He gave His only begotten Son, that whoever believes in Him should not perish but have everlasting life.

For God so loved the world... He set us free from the power of sin. He does not just set us free and then leave us face to face with this sinful world. The entire Old Testament demonstrates the fact that it is impossible for a man to free himself from vices. Adam sinned and died. Sin was crouching at the door of Cain (Genesis 4:7). What can be said about the following generations? Every time they sinned they kept bringing goats and lambs as sacrifices so that diseases and weaknesses would not destroy their bodies. The blood of the sacrifices only covered over the sins in the flesh and as a result a temporary healing would come. But the blood of animals could not clear man's conscience and so the sin would return, bodies became destroyed, souls remained sick. Draw a parallel between that time and today. What has changed? We keep going to doctors, we keep sacrificing our time and bringing offerings...so that we could stay alive. Neither medicine nor surgeries can make your body perfect. It does not matter how good the prosthesis is, it will never be better than a natural organ. Sacrificial offerings are going on even today...

There was no sacrifice on earth the blood of which was not tainted by sin. The entire world lay in sin. The entire world was subject to the curse. The sinful nature was passed down from fathers to children in the blood. And so the sin was passed on. This was going on until Jesus Christ, the Son of God, came. He was conceived by the Holy Spirit and His blood was not tainted with sin. He came to offer His Blood as a sacrifice for our sins.

**1Peter 2:24
...who Himself bore our sins in His own body on the tree, that we, having died to sins, might live for righteousness — by whose stripes you were healed.

Where there is redemption from sins there is no place for sickness, disease, poverty or any other curses.

**Psalm 107:17-21
17. Fools, because of their transgression, And because of their iniquities, were afflicted.
18. Their soul abhorred all manner of food, And they drew near to the gates of death.

19. Then they cried out to the LORD in their trouble, And He saved them out of their distresses.
20. He sent His word and healed them, And delivered them from their destructions.
21. Oh, that men would give thanks to the LORD for His goodness, And for His wonderful works to the children of men!

"He sent His Word". Who is the Word? Jesus is the Word of God. God sent Him in human form to become the sacrifice of atonement for our sins. The sacrificed was offered. We have been redeemed. We are now free.

**Hebrews 10:10
10. By that will we have been sanctified through the offering of the body of Jesus Christ once for all.

By the sacrifice of Jesus Christ we are saved from everlasting torments, from hell; we are healed from sickness and disease. There is no curse that He has not redeemed us from. None of Satan's weapons have power over us or our families. Jesus gave us the authority, and the Holy Spirit teaches us how to use it. He teaches us to trust in the word and to live by faith not by sight. He teaches us to walk in divine health which was paid for by the Blood.

**John 8:31
Then Jesus said to those Jews who believed Him, "If you abide in My word, you are My disciples indeed.

**John 15:7
7. If you abide in Me, and My words abide in you, you will[b] ask what you desire, and it shall be done for you.

**1John 2:24
24. Therefore let that abide in you which you heard from the beginning. If what you heard from the beginning abides in you, you also will abide in the Son and in the Father.

Abiding in the Word means spending time with God. When we become absorbed in the Bible, the Holy Spirit reveals to us the secrets which are hidden in the Word of God. He opens up the truth which makes us free from any disorders of this world. He has already separated us from this world, where the evil rules. We must learn to rule over it, for Jesus has given us the authority over demons, diseases and death. Unless we use that authority, Satan will use it. Everyone who follows Christ must study the Scriptures: God gave us the power and authority to live a victorious life. With this power we become invulnerable to sin. We can resist sin, because its power was destroyed on Calvary. If we know the truth and trust in the Word, we use the authority which has been given to us. We die for sin to walk in the truth. If we walk in His light, all darkness with its evil and disease is forced to give up.

**<u>Romans 6:2</u>
Certainly not! How shall we who died to sin live any longer in it?

God gave us the power to resist sin and live a righteous life. This power is in the Holy Spirit. When we are obedient to the Spirit of God, humble in our heart, and seek His face – we are under His power. He educates and teaches us. He teaches us not to sin. He rebukes us. We can hear His voice when we are attentive to Him and when we abide in His presence. But when we drift apart from Him carried away by everyday fuss, His place is taken by the worldly spirit. And we become vulnerable to sin and consequently to diseases.

**<u>Galatians 5:16</u>
16. I say then: Walk in the Spirit, and you shall not fulfill the lust of the flesh.

**<u>James 4:7,8,11</u>
7. Therefore submit to God. Resist the devil and he will flee from you.
8. Draw near to God and He will draw near to you. Cleanse your hands, you sinners; and purify your hearts, you double-minded.
11. Do not speak evil of one another, brethren.

We can read the teaching of the Holy Spirit in the epistle of James, from the beginning to the end, until this word is embodied in us, until our flesh dies to the sin under this word. And we know that the word is always living. It works according to what it carries. The word of cleansing cleanses us, the word of healing heals us. Until we let the inner processes be run their full course, it is unlikely that anything will radically change.

Father God desires with all His heart that we were transformed into His holy image. His life is running through our new nature. He accepts us unconditionally the way we are. We are baptized in Jesus. He accepts us in His Son Jesus Christ. We absorb Him, and the ocean of God's love polishes us, daily washing away any accumulated rubbish, and makes us the way we are supposed to be.

Holiness means to live for the Lord. We cannot allow ourselves to live the way other people live in this world. It takes effort and perseverance to resist the temptations and rules of this world. It is a process which last our entire lifetime on this earth.

Thanks to Jesus, Who has redeemed us, we remain God's children even if we sin. Jesus will always be our Healer.

> ****_1John 2:1_**
> **_My little children, these things I write to you, so that you may not sin. And if anyone sins, we have an Advocate with the Father, Jesus Christ the righteous._**

If having fallen into sin we sincerely repent, we will not lose our salvation. The Blood of Jesus washes away all sin and destroys the memory of this sin as if it has never happened.

> ****_Jeremiah 31:34_**
> **_...I will forgive their iniquity, and their sin I will remember no more._"**

> ****_1John 1:9_**
> **_If we confess our sins, He is faithful and just to forgive us our sins and to cleanse us from all unrighteousness._**

Jesus as our High Priest appeals for us before Father. He, our Lord, has the everlasting authority to forgive our sins. Where sins are forgiven there is healing from disease.

Jesus forgave the sins of the man in Bethesda, otherwise the healing would not have happened. That is why Jesus said: "Sin no more". If the root of disease, the sin- is destroyed, the disease itself will be destroyed as well. We read that the man had been suffering from the consequences of his sins for 38 years before he met the One Who had the authority to forgive sins. And that encounter radically changed his life. He experienced the miracle of healing. And what happened next? Jesus found him in the temple and warned: "Sin no more, lest a worse thing come upon you."

God forgives us for good. He is so merciful! His love for us is so great! So unconditional! Our mind cannot understand it, but we can trust it.

You have probably made a mistake: you have not forgiven someone, have offended someone, have doubted, have become irritated, quarreled with someone, put your hope in someone... You cannot even imagine how close to you loving and almighty God was that moment and He had already His answer for you. You probably ignored God who knocked your heart, did not you? You did not do anything wrong to anybody just lived for yourself. But if you have not given your life to Jesus and you are in this world, you have to know that Satan rules over this world. He has all rights to your life. What can you do? Cross over into the cover of the mighty hand of God! He is waiting for you. Repent! Otherwise the disease will use any reason to enter into your body and destroy it. Sin is all the cause and invitation it needs.

I say with Peter's words:

**_Acts 2:37,38_
37. Now when they heard this, they were cut to the heart, and said to Peter and the rest of the apostles, "Men and brethren, what shall we do?"
38. Then Peter said to them, "Repent, and let every one of you be baptized in the name of Jesus Christ for the remission of sins; and you shall receive the gift of the Holy Spirit.

Be free from sins! God says that He is ready to forgive you! Why do you have to carry the consequences of sins? Why do you have to suffer from disease? Repent so that He could reveal His healing power. God cares for our healing so much that He can stop the sun and the moon and make the shadow cast by the sun go back ten steps... He loves to answer our prayers so much!

**James 4:8
8. Draw near to God and He will draw near to you. Cleanse your hands, you sinners; and purify your hearts, you double-minded.

Draw near to God. In His presence no sin will survive. You will become free. The Holy Spirit, Who has been given to us as a promise, will teach us to live righteously so that we could receive our healing, hold on to it, stay healthy and sin no more. Repentance means to turn around and go in the opposite direction, far away from sin. We have received forgiveness of sins and a place among those who are sanctified by faith in Jesus. But we can lose it if we lead a sinful way of life.

If a man sins again and again, he eventually stops hearing the conviction of the Holy Spirit. Then his heart turns to stone.

**Hebrews 10:26
26. For if we sin willfully after we have received the knowledge of the truth, there no longer remains a sacrifice for sins,

This is the most terrible thing that can happen, because God can fix and heal the rest, even create something new. Hell is a real place. It is the eternal place of torment and horror.

From the book of John G. Lake "The power above demons, diseases and death" (page 62)
During the prayer be broken in spirit and do not hold back your tears. If your prayers are so deep that they make you cry it means that God is seeking the way to get into your life. Who of you confessed your sins while you were praying for your healing? Who asked for help to

become free from sins and was sincere in his request? Who put himself upon God's altar with his full awareness of the decision? Only such acts open the way for God. God's chariot can speed freely along the road of your life if all rocks are taken away. May the Lord be blessed!

Let us pray together:

Lord Jesus! I believe that You have paid for all my sins with Your Blood. You have closed the way to disease and other curses of this world into my life. Now my life belongs to You, Lord. Fill it with Your light. Cast out any thorns out of my mind. Renew my mind. I believe that You cherish me as the apple of Your eye. See if there is any offensive way in me so that You could return me onto the way of Your truth. "Cleanse me with hyssop, and I will be clean; wash me, and I will be whiter than snow" (**Psalm 51:7).

John G. Lake prayed this way: "Give me strength to do right things, and if I have done something evil, let me repent, confess and be restored whatever it costs".

Amen!

Chapter 11

Where two or three
are gathered together

Mathew 18:20
*For where two or three are gathered together in My name, I am there
in the midst of them."*

The Lord said:"Where two or three are gathered together...". He sees
us victorious in the power of unanimity. We always influence by the spirit.
The question is, what spirit do we unite and influence one another in? As
long as "the Spirit of the Sovereign Lord is on me", then everything is all
right. We are the organism of Jesus Christ, His Body. His Blood circulates
in us, as we are united by one Spirit. His blood cleanses us, washes away
any foreign things and pushes out the secular spirit which, like the thorns
of the proverb, muffles the word of life and victory in Christ.

Numbers 14:24
*But My servant Caleb, because he has a different spirit in him and
has followed Me fully, I will bring into the land where he went, and his
descendants shall inherit it.*

**<u>Numbers 14:38</u>
**38. But Joshua the son of Nun and Caleb the son of Jephunneh re-
mained alive, of the men who went to spy out the land.**

They survived, because they had a different spirit. They let the
Spirit of God control their thoughts and feelings. They trusted God
more than their own eyes. They looked at the land God offered them
through His eyes, the eyes of faith. The rest of the people lived by visible things. They talked about the situation according to what their
frightened eyes saw and did not believe in the possibility of victory.
But the victory had already been prepared. Why would God allow defeat, when He had already planned the victory? He just needed the
people who would step up and claim it. He offered the people of Israel
a battle of faith. Everyone had a choice: to trust God or that which
their eyes were seeing, to proclaim what they saw or to admit the Word
of God.

**<u>Numbers 14:28,37</u>
**28. Say to them, 'As I live,' says the LORD, 'just as you have spo-
ken in My hearing, so I will do to you:
37. those very men who brought the evil report about the land, died
by the plague before the LORD.**

"The evil report" means the words which do not correspond to the
Word of God. Have faith in God! What company of people have you
joined today? The society will be always divided into groups of people
who live by faith and who live by what they see. Visible things say:
"You have a terminal disease. You will die". Faith says: "It is written
that, "by His stripes I am healed"". I choose to believe the Word of
God despite what I may see or feel. All visible things are temporary.
All my symptoms are temporary. My healing is real! It is mine! I believe that I have it even now, not when my body finally admits it.

There will always be different destinies. Those who live by faith
have a different spirit. This spirit sees with the eyes of God.

From the article of Gloria Copeland "Communicate with those who are faithful" (the magazine "Believer's Voice of Victory", 2008, April-May, page 5).

If you want to live in victory, you need to communicate with people who know God. Do not try to communicate with the world and live victoriously at the same time. It will not work. We receive strength from each another. We receive weakness from each other as well. If you want to become stronger, find some people who are stronger in the Lord than you and communicate with them. They will lift you up. But if you communicate with people who do not live for God and do not trust His Word, they will bring you down.

**2Thessalinians 3:1,2
1. Finally, brethren, pray for us, that the word of the Lord may run swiftly and be glorified, just as it is with you,
2. and that we may be delivered from unreasonable and wicked men; for not all have faith.

If you surround yourself with people who are in a constant search for doctors, always talk about their disease and are convinced that divine healing is a thing of the past, do not even try to retain your divine health. It will simply not work. If you contribute to these conversations, you have become a part of it. Sickness and disease love to have to have you for company. Doubt walks closely with disbelief, disbelief is a friend of anxiety, and anxiety provokes fear. Fear, in turn, opens the door for unclean and evil things. We step out of God's territory when we let the fear affect us: "I am afraid I am getting sick!... It is terrifying to think how many people have been affected by this flu!" Yes, many people may have, but this flu will not come near you. God promises: IT SHALL NOT COME NEAR YOU!

**Psalm 91:7
7. A thousand may fall at your side, and ten thousand at your right hand; but it shall not come near you.

Do not look for those who will feel sorry for you and are ready to weep with you, those who doubt... Jesus did not permit the mourners to be where the miracles of God were happening. Stick close to those people who live by faith, strong Christians, who give praise to God, who confess the word of victory. The power of the healing Spirit of God comes to places where words of victory and faith are spoken. Demons are drawn to the spirit of disbelief and anxiety. Link up your shield of faith with the shields of those who know for certain what God's promises regarding sickness, disease, demons and death in your life. And the Lord will stand among you as the Great Witness and Lawmaker and He will multiply the power of life in you. Even two people are enough for the darkness to step back...

**Ecclesiastes 4:12
12. Though one may be overpowered by another, two can withstand him. And a threefold cord is not quickly broken.

**1John 1:7
7. But if we walk in the light as He is in the light, we have fellowship with one another, and the blood of Jesus Christ His Son cleanses us from all sin.

Our enemy dwells in the invisible realm. The weapons we fight with are not of this world but they are powerful... He who has eyes let him see. He who does not have wisdom to see let him ask God, Who will answer, and not judge anyone. But if you ask, you must believe without a doubt – this is the condition of God (**James 1:5-8). If you are bold enough to believe in what you do not see, then do not doubt. Whatever you ask God for, He will give it to you from the invisible realm. And you must receive it by faith. The righteous will live by faith. We can walk by faith, because we are baptized with the Holy Spirit. He teaches us. When victory seems out of reach, we activate our faith in the invisible and then the impossible will happen.

**Ephesians 4:3
...endeavoring to keep the unity of the Spirit in the bond of peace.

When we pray together, we put everything in action. We put the law of spirit of life in action. The word we release, always acts and accomplishes what it was sent for. That is why we can say after every prayer:"It has happened!" We affirm our healing, prosperity, salvation of our children... At that moment Jesus stands in our midst.

> ****Mathew 18:19-20*
> *19. "Again I say[c] to you that if two of you agree on earth concerning anything that they ask, it will be done for them by My Father in heaven.*
> *20. For where two or three are gathered together in My name, I am there in the midst of them."*

He is in our midst, and therefore our power is limitless. Carefully chose those who you are going to pray in agreement with.

> ****Acts 4:31*
> *31. And when they had prayed, the place where they were assembled together was shaken; and they were all filled with the Holy Spirit, and they spoke the word of God with boldness.*

A great power was with them. The same power acts within us now. Satan cannot conquer us, because God with us. The One Who is in you is greater than the one who is in the world. We receive it by faith.

Raise your shield of faith. Link up your shield with the shields of those, who trust God with their divine health, who walk with power, who live according to the Word and receive answers to their prayers. When warriors link up their shields and act in one accord, they make a solid armour, impenetrable to any arrow.

A scene from the film "Gladiator": a battle of gladiators in the arena of the Coliseum. The ticket price for their death has already been paid. Everything is set up in the way that every gladiator would be killed. The fighters are slaves. They are under control of the forces of darkness. There is nothing to turn the odds around. But! The situation spins out of control when one of the condemned men decides to resist the planned scenario. This man is a former Roman army general, who was taught to fight and win. This man assumes the power over the situation and turns the planned defeat into their victory. He tells his fellow gladiators: "We can win if we are together as one". Thus, as one, they link up their shields and the arrows of the enemies cannot go through this armour. Those under the iron cover of shields survive. Those who are not are killed instantly.

Therefore, if your shield is a shield of faith, no weapon forged against you will prevail. Jesus, the Word of God, promises that. If we link up our shields as one, we will become stronger and will act. Then whatever darkness is advancing, it will step back and vanish like a fog as if it never existed. All visible things are temporary.

**_Leviticus 26:8_
8. Five of you shall chase a hundred, and a hundred of you shall put ten thousand to flight; your enemies shall fall by the sword before you.

From the book of Kenneth E. Hagen "The Holy Spirit and His gifts" (page 6).
Fellowship with those who believe in the things precious to you helps you to grow spiritually, just like medication helps overcome the disease. I have built my faith this way.

Pray with me.
Father! I entrust my life to You, every following day and year of my life. I ask You for wisdom in all my actions, decisions and deeds.

Dear Holy Spirit! Lead me and teach me. I want to receive and learn from You, just like all the men and women of faith, of whom I read in the Bible, learned from You. You say in Your Word that Your sheep know Your voice and do not follow the voice of another. Teach me to hear You, and to be always sensitive to Your voice.

Surround me with the people who know You and believe in Your divine health for everyone who calls upon Your mighty name. Teach me to recognize those who are deceived. Teach me to recognize the true teaching.

Lord, prepare me for my ministry. I ask You to give me the experience and the ability to be the answer to people's needs. If I work in a team of people, with whom You will join me in Your power, teach me "to keep the unity of the Spirit in the bond of peace" in the name of Jesus!
Amen!

Chapter 12

Why does it seem that your prayer goes unanswered?

Habakkuk 1:2
O LORD, how long shall I cry, and You will not hear? Even cry out to You, "Violence!" And You will not save.

Why are some people healed, but other people are not? Why does one person survive after being in the last phase of cancer, and another dies after the first phase? Why do we need to wait so long to be healed? Can't God heal me at once? Why must I suffer so much? Is it God's will? Why does not He answer my prayers? Why?! Why?!..

We need to look for the answer in the Word of God. We need a foundation that will give us the confidence in our prayers. We need to put the Bible before our eyes and "taste and see that the Lord is good". Let us examine the Bible and talk about the prayer of healing. Healing is God's will. Whether we talk about prosperity or salvation of our children, or a good relationship in our family, we will use the same method when teaching about healing.

1. ****_Hebrews 11:6_**
But without faith it is impossible to please Him, for he who comes to God must believe that He is, and that He is a rewarder of those who diligently seek Him.

It does not matter whether you are relying on the doctors for help or you believe in God's miracles, the healing comes from God! The man cannot heal. He can only perform the physical work, therapy, surgery, or prescribe a treatment.

> *From the book of Katherine Kulman "I believe in miracles" (page 12):*
> *The doctor who enters the room of the sick is not alone. He can serve those who are in need with the instruments of scientific medicine. His faith in superior power does the rest.*
> *..."All healings have divine nature" – said Doctor Elmer Gess.*
> *A doctor can fix a broken bone, but it will heal under the influence of divine power. A surgeon can perform the most complex surgery, he can be a real master of the scalpel and use the most advanced knowledge, but then he has to wait while the superior power accomplishes the real healing. People do not possess the ability to heal.*

There are always two ways: to look for a doctor or to seek God's face. If you have dared to put your hope in God and pray to Him, you need faith. "But without faith it is impossible to please Him, for he who comes to God must believe that He is, and that He is a rewarder of those who diligently seek Him." He rewards you with healing according to your faith. There are three points of instruction in these verses:

a) to come to God (with all your heart);
b) to believe in Him;
c) to seek Him.

This is the process.

God provides a way for us to have faith. He tells us in His Word how to receive faith so that we could receive our healing.

2. **Romans 10:17
So then faith comes by hearing, and hearing by the word of God.

It is not enough to hear once that God is the Healer. It is written: "faith comes by hearing, and hearing by the word of God." Faith comes to us by hearing. And I would add that faith also comes by seeing the word, because we hear the word, read the word, and therefore we see it. It is written that "hearing is by the word of God". What sort of hearing? How does it happen?

You put the Word of God (the Bible) before your eyes, confess it with your mouth and hear it with your ears. You take it like you would take your medicine. The word, which is living and active, penetrates you and accomplishes its perfect works in you. And that is a process. The word is a seed (Mark 4). You feed your spirit with it. You let the word germinate in you. When it roots itself in your heart or in your spirit, and germinates, this living word begins to speak to your mind. You begin to hear the voice of God from within you and after that you become absolutely certain that healing belongs to you in spite of all the symptoms and physical signs. This is the faith, which comes by hearing. And it comes from the Word. It is pity that people search for their healing everywhere except in God's Word. While it is so easy to fill their eyes and ears with the Word. The Word is the beginning. It will bring faith to you. You will be able to move the mountain of any disease by your faith. You need to grow in the faith. It takes time. Do not waste it!

3. **James 5:14,15
14. Is anyone among you sick? Let him call for the elders of the church, and let them pray over him, anointing him with oil in the name of the Lord.
15. And the prayer of faith will save the sick, and the Lord will raise him up. And if he has committed sins, he will be forgiven.

If you know that your faith is still growing, and you have just begun learning to believe God, and it is difficult for you to take a stand with strong faith, then act wisely — call the elders of the church who believe in divine healing. If there is any sin in your life, remember: when you confess, God loves to forgive and heal your heart. When He forgives, He heals, and when He heals, He forgives. Otherwise no one would be healed, because disease is from sin. The following Scripture will encourage you.

**Isaiah 43:25
25. "I, even I, am He who blots out your transgressions for My own sake; And I will not remember your sins.

4. ****James 5:16**
Confess your trespasses[e] to one another, and pray for one another, that you may be healed. The effective, fervent prayer of a righteous man avails much.

Bring before Him everything that concerns you. Confess your sin, bring out all unrighteousness. Our God is the God of order and peace. Our God is merciful. He will put everything in order and give peace to your heart.

**1John 1:9
9. If we confess our sins, He is faithful and just to forgive us our sins and to cleanse us from all unrighteousness.

We must believe God's forgiveness just as we believe His healing. There is no need for us to carry around the burden of guilt, because the merciful God is not going to remind us of our past. Confess, accept forgiveness from the Father and be well again!

5. ****Mathew 18:19,20**
19. "Again I say[c] to you that if two of you agree on earth concerning anything that they ask, it will be done for them by My Father in heaven.
20. For where two or three are gathered together in My name, I am there in the midst of them."

Praying in Agreement.

From the book of Kenneth E. Hagen "The Basics of Spiritual Growth" (Lesson 31. Prayer of agreement)

The prayer in agreement of two or more people about any need has great power.

...There is no promise in the Bible more important than Mathew 18:19.

...Take note of the verse 19: "it will be done for them by my Father in Heaven". He also said: "You may ask Me for anything in My name, and I will do it" (**John 14:14).

P. Nelson was an expert of the Greek language who read the New Testament only in Greek.

Dr. Nelson said that Jesus' words in Greek are literally mean the following: "You may ask Me for anything, and if I do not have it, I will create it for you".

You can act alone or ask for help. An example of a joint prayer is described in the book of Acts:

**Acts 4:31
31. And when they had prayed, the place where they were assembled together was shaken; and they were all filled with the Holy Spirit, and they spoke the word of God with boldness.

The great power was with them. The same power acts within you to-day. Satan cannot conquer us, because God is with us. The One Who is in you is greater than the one who is in the world. We accept it by faith.

Choose wisely the people who you are going to pray with. Je-sus did not allow mourners to be present in the place where God's miracles were happening.

6. **Mark 11:23-26
23. For assuredly, I say to you, whoever says to this mountain, 'Be removed and be cast into the sea,' and does not doubt in his heart, but believes that those things he says will be done, he will have whatever he says.

24. Therefore I say to you, whatever things you ask when you pray, believe that you receive them, and you will have them.
25. "And whenever you stand praying, if you have anything against anyone, forgive him, that your Father in heaven may also forgive you your trespasses. 26 But if you do not forgive, neither will your Father in heaven forgive your trespasses."

Let us examine this verse of the Scripture closely. It teaches us how to ask for something in prayer:

A.) We must believe that we will receive. Not when we finally see the result, but from the very moment we begin asking, even as we are praying for it. When we are ready to believe, then we receive right away; the miracle happens. Sometimes it takes time for the answer to our prayer to transfer from the invisible spiritual realm into the physical one that is visible. It happens when we pray. (It was in this way that a man in Lystra received the use of his legs in the Book of Acts 14:8-10.)

B.) Another thing we must draw from **Mark 11:23-26, is- do not doubt when you ask. God is not like a man to deceive. We must trust Him absolutely.

**Mark 11:24
24. Therefore I say to you, whatever things you ask when you pray, believe that you receive them, and you will have them.

It is written in the Scripture about those who doubt:

**James 1:6-8
6. But let him ask in faith, with no doubting, for he who doubts is like a wave of the sea driven and tossed by the wind.
7. For let not that man suppose that he will receive anything from the Lord;
8. he is a double-minded man, unstable in all his ways.

Therefore how should we ask God? With certainty that we receive what we ask. Say out loud: "My healing is here! The Heavenly Father wants to see me healthy and whole! I have it even now. Thank You, Father!" It does not matter what your body says to you at that moment. It must and will listen to what you say to it. Your words must be in accordance to God's teaching about healing. And you will have His faith so that you could receive from Him what you ask.

C.) What else do we need to do? Forgive!

Mark 11:25,26
25. "And whenever you stand praying, if you have anything against anyone, forgive him, so that your Father in heaven may also forgive you your trespasses.
26. But if you do not forgive, neither will your Father in heaven forgive your trespasses."

Unforgiveness blocks our prayer. Set yourself free of this feeling, because it eats up your soul n the same way as cancer eats up the body. Unforgiveness separates us from God. It is not harmless. It destroys us. We will have to root out everything that has been sowed from this world. "I am too proud, so I will not be the first to approach him!",..."If you only knew how she has offended me!" We are used to behaving ourselves like "regular" people, but God sees it differently. He opposes the proud. Tell me, what good is pride if we lose God's grace because of it? God makes us an offer: if I forgive my offender, God promises to forgives my sins. I cannot afford to feel offended. Any unforgiveness is a sin. As a consequence of unforgiveness a disease has a right to invade the body. Do you really want to let it? Forgive everyone in any situation.

D.) What else do we need? To speak to the mountain.

Mark 11:23
23. For assuredly, I say to you, whoever says to this mountain, 'Be removed and be cast into the sea,' and does not doubt in his heart, but believes that those things he says will be done, he will have whatever he says.

Proclaim your deliverance according to the Word. You need to speak the words of faith aloud. It is a confession of faith. We say it into the physical world with our physical mouth, addressing a physical problem.

**Psalm 91:9,10
Because you have made the LORD, who is my refuge, even the Most High, your dwelling place, no evil shall befall you, nor shall any plague come near your dwelling.

7. Let us look at the classic example of prayer from the mouth of God Himself - Jesus. This prayer is known to all. Even people who have never opened the Bible know the prayer "Our Father".

**Mathew 6:9-13
9. In this manner, therefore, pray: Our Father in heaven, Hallowed be Your name.
10. Your kingdom come. Your will be done On earth as it is in heaven.
11. Give us this day our daily bread.
12. And forgive us our debts, As we forgive our debtors.
13. And do not lead us into temptation, But deliver us from the evil one. For Yours is the kingdom and the power and the glory forever. Amen.

Even so, it is only a part of what Jesus taught about prayer. The entire sixth chapter of the Gospel of Mathew is about Jesus teaching His disciples how to communicate with the Father.

A) **Mathew 6:3,4
But when you do a charitable deed, do not let your left hand know what your right hand is doing, that your charitable deed may be in secret; and your Father who sees in secret will Himself reward you openly.

Scripture says, "That your charitable deed may be"... It must be. We cannot but give. Giving is the nature of God. He gave His Son. What can prevent us from giving? Giving is a requirement, not a suggestion. The Father gives to us, when He sees us giving and doing charitable works.

B) **Mathew 6:5,6
"And when you pray, you shall not be like the hypocrites. For they love to pray standing in the synagogues and on the corners of the streets, that they may be seen by men. Assuredly, I say to you, they have their reward.

It should not matter to us how we look, but rather how we look in God's eyes. We always have a grand audience in the Person of One (God).

But you, when you pray, go into your room, and when you have shut your door, pray to your Father who is in the secret place; and your Father who sees in secret will reward you openly.

We must spend our prayer time with the Father in a secret place. We have no right to deny Him our time. Prayer and fellowship with God is not a ritual. It is not a public act. It is a question of a close and personal relationship that grows in direct proportion to the amount of time we spend time with Him. We can share our secrets with Him. He will, in turn, reveal His secrets to us. It is between Him and us. It is very personal... and the most important thing in our life.

C.) **Mathew 6:7,8
And when you pray, do not use vain repetitions as the heathen do. For they think that they will be heard for their many words. "Therefore do not be like them. For your Father knows the things you have need of before you ask Him.

God knows everything. We know little. He knows what we are going to pray about before we utter the first word and before we even think about it. We must be sincere, the way children are, telling God everything that is in our heart. It is easy for little children to communicate with their parents.

They do not stop to think about ways of approaching their mother or father. They simply talk about their needs. A relationship with God is fairly simple. Why then do we make it so complicated?

> *D.) **Mathew 6:16-18*
> *16. "Moreover, when you fast, do not be like the hypocrites, with a sad countenance. For they disfigure their faces that they may appear to men to be fasting. Assuredly, I say to you, they have their reward.*
> *17. But you, when you fast, anoint your head and wash your face,*
> *18. so that you do not appear to men to be fasting, but to your Father who is in the secret place; and your Father who sees in secret will reward you openly.*

This verse speaks about fasting, which means giving up food and other things of habit. Fasting helps us become closer to God at the moment of our prayer. We restrain our flesh which resists the spirit. We humble ourselves in fast and prayer, so that we could receive from God's Spirit into our own all the answers to our questions. When we practice fasting and prayer, our faith is able to reaches things which surpass our understanding. Be sure of it:

> ***Mathew 17:20,21*
> *So Jesus said to them, "Because of your unbelief; for assuredly, I say to you, if you have faith as a mustard seed, you will say to this mountain, 'Move from here to there,' and it will move; and nothing will be impossible for you. However, this kind does not go out except by prayer and fasting."*

For us as well, nothing will be impossible, if we fast regularly, according to Jesus' instructions. It is the supernatural means given to us by God, which makes it easier for our prayers to get answered. We may have an urgent need that we turn to God for, such as praying for someone who is in the last phase of a terminal illness. Learn more about fasting. It opens up an absolutely different level of life in God.

**Isaiah 65:24
24. " It shall come to pass that before they call, I will answer; and while they are still speaking, I will hear.

Fasting does not change God. Fasting does not change Satan's plans to kill you. Fasting will change you. It will change you in such a way that you will reach a level of the supernatural, where nothing will be impossible for you. Fasting will take away all power of disease and demonic power.

Let fasting become a regular part of your life!

E.)**Mathew 6:19,20
19 "Do not lay up for yourselves treasures on earth, where moth and rust destroy and where thieves break in and steal; 20 but lay up for yourselves treasures in heaven, where neither moth nor rust destroys and where thieves do not break in and steal.

Where is your treasure? Who is your treasure? Where is your heart? Who is your heart with? What does it long for? What fills it? What are your values? Is it difficult for you to go through the eye of a needle? (**Mathew 19:24, **Mark 10:25, **Luke 18:25)

If you put God and His Word first, you will not need to spend a long time, praying and fasting, asking Him to solve your problems. You will replace your prayers of requests with the prayers of thanksgiving.

8. *In summary.*

**Mathew 6:31-34
31. "Therefore do not worry, saying, 'What shall we eat?' or 'What shall we drink?' or 'What shall we wear?'
32. For after all these things the Gentiles seek. For your heavenly Father knows that you need all these things.
33. But seek first the kingdom of God and His righteousness, and all these things shall be added to you.
34. Therefore do not worry about tomorrow, for tomorrow will worry about its own things. Sufficient for the day is its own trouble.

Worries, anxiety, fear of the future... That is not faith. It is the disbelief of the world. Fuss. But we are in the shelter of the Most High, and thus always have a peace of mind. Therefore – always trust God and His Word.

9. One other important point.

Romans 8:26,27
26. Likewise the Spirit also helps in our weaknesses. For we do not know what we should pray for as we ought, but the Spirit Himself makes intercession for us[b] with groanings which cannot be uttered.
27. Now He who searches the hearts knows what the mind of the Spirit is, because He makes intercession for the saints according to the will of God.

1Corinthians 14:15
What is the conclusion then? I will pray with the spirit, and I will also pray with the understanding. I will sing with the spirit, and I will also sing with the understanding.

If you have not received the Holy Spirit (I am talking about baptizm in the Holy Spirit and speaking in tongues), you do not have the power.

Acts 1:8
8. But you shall receive power when the Holy Spirit has come upon you; and you shall be witnesses to Me[a] in Jerusalem, and in all Judea and Samaria, and to the end of the earth. "

Our own strength is not enough. The Holy Spirit gives us the power from Heaven. He opens the Scripture to us. He intercedes for us. He edifies us. He teaches us. He gives us His gifts. We become strong when we are taught by God's Holy Spirit. Paul wrote that he spoke tongues more than anyone else. That is why he ended up writing the biggest part of the New Testament. Through Apostle Paul, the Holy Spirit imparted many valuable lessons to the mankind.

10. *******Jeremiah 33:2,3***
"Thus says the LORD who made it, the LORD who formed it to estab-
lish it (the LORD is His name): 'Call to Me, and I will answer you,
and show you great and mighty things, which you do not know.'

God loves us as His children. He calls us to speak to Him. We will never
cope with our problems on our own. We must always ask Him for help. He
loves to answer our prayers. Our prayer is when we talk to Him. He loves
to make us happy, to reveal His magnificence to us... He is ready to share
His secrets with us!.. He is the God of miracles!.. Only we must believe in
Him! He guarantees that He will answers us. He speaks so much about
it! (**Mathew 7:7, **Mathew 21:22, **Luke 11:9, **John 14:13, **John
14:14, **John 15:7, **John 15:16, **John 16:23, **John 16:24)

John 16:24
24. Until now you have asked nothing in My name. Ask, and you will
receive, that your joy may be full.

11. Are there any other reasons why prayers can go unanswered?

James 4:3
3. You ask and do not receive, because you ask amiss, that you may
spend it on your pleasures.

Study the Scriptures. Hold fast to His teaching day and night, so that
you would know what is good and what is bad, according to God. Learn
to do what God instructs. As we learn the truth, our souls and our bodies
are healed. We become different. We become the way He sees us.

12. And finally.

"The secret things belong to the LORD our God, but those things
which are revealed belong to us and to our children forever, that we may
do all the words of this law..." (**Deuteronomy 29:29)

There is something that God leaves unrevealed. There are some secrets which we are not ready or would not be able to accept. Allow for certain questions to remain open for the time being.

Some day "whether there are prophecies, they will fail; whether there are tongues, they will cease; whether there is knowledge, it will vanish away" (**1Corinthians 13:8) and we will get to Heaven and ask the Father all of our questions face to face. He will reveal Himself to us, and we will see.

> ****1Corinthians 13:12**
> *12 For now we see in a mirror, dimly, but then face to face. Now I know in part, but then I shall know just as I also am known.*

I want to tell you one story.

In 2005 I was diagnosed with cancer. I was undergoing the traditional prescribed treatment in the oncology center. Although there was little to no hope that I would live, the doctors had to prescribe the usual treatment and they did their job. In the meantime I buried myself deeper and deeper into the Scripture.

Every day I was surrounded by people who were diagnosed with the same incurable disease. I did my best to reach out to everyone I met. I was not as confident as I am today of God's will for healing. But I knew Him as my Saviour and my Redeemer. I testified how God had healed me from an incurable disease in my past. I believed that God has not changed. I prayed for everyone I met. I laid my hands on them and did not mind the frequent question: "If your God heals, then why are you here?" At night, when everyone was asleep, I put drops of anointing oil on the sides and tops of the doorframes of the wards, where people were dying, and kept on praying.

One night while I was walking along the corridor I saw a figure approaching me. It was hard to tell whether it was a man or a woman. I just saw a body of a person, wheezing and doubled up with pain. It was a barefooted woman who could hardly walk. She did not care how she looked. Cancer was killing any perception of life in her.

I stopped her and asked: "Will you let me pray for you?" She lifted her pain filled eyes and wheezed: "I have been waiting for you!.. You prayed for me in the elevator... I have been waiting for you...". I told her about

God, Who took up our infirmities and carried our diseases. She did not ask me provocative questions like "Why are you here?" She was listening to me openly. The pain seemed to stop tormenting her. She said the Sinner's Prayer so sincerely! She cried and said: "If God delivers me from death, I will serve only Him for the rest of my life".

In the morning I was told that one gravely sick patient was being moved into my hospital room. There were only two beds. I embraced the empty bed with all of my body and prayed for the patient who was coming... Very soon the woman who I had talked to the previous night was brought to my ward. She was hooked up to an oxygen tank. She was dying... She said: "I asked God that I could see you again. You are like an angel to me now". I laid my hands upon her. Suddenly her face began to shine! It was shining as if someone covered her with sparkling mica. It was not a vision. It was a physical manifestation of God's touch. The only thing I could think of was that God was letting her live. That He was healing her. There were no other thoughts except one: she will live!..

The next day she was moved to another wing. A few days later I learned that she died...

"The secret things belong to the Lord our God". There was peace in my heart. I knew why: she did not go to hell. Like an interceptor, a border patrol guard on the border of life and death at the last moment I put her into God's hands. He accepted her. Why did not He leave her on this earth to serve Him? I do not know. I only saw how He touched her and gave her freedom. Why did it happen in such a way?.. "The secret things belong to the Lord our God". But the most important thing took place. She will spend the eternity in the place where there is no pain, no tears, no fears and no sorrows. I thank my God for using me to save one soul.

Afterword

After you read this book, you will understand that this is just the beginning, but this beginning is the right one. It is the way of healing that God Himself has prepared for us.

This book is just a small part of what I want to share with you about the divine healing and what God has revealed to me. He has revelations that are meant specifically for you. There are more revelations than you can imagine, and they cannot be all fitted into any book, except for one. All God's revelations, all the recipes for healing that He has prepared for you, all the amazing and original ways of divine healing are contained in the one and only source, the Bible, the Book for your life, where every word is living.

It is His foundation. God Himself is the Word. You can build your life on Him; a life without weakness, disease, disappointment and failure...

Your Almighty Healer is waiting for you to come in contact with His Word, so that He could guide you and lead you out of any problem, any diagnosis, and bring you to victory over weakness, illness and death. He is waiting for you to choose a path. Choose His way, the way of life. Trust Him. He is ready to give you what He has prepared, to give you what you need. "Come to Me, all you who are weary and burdened, and I will give you rest". (**Mathew 11:28)

You need to be at peace and allow God, as the divine Doctor, to intervene in your life.

Be still and watch God's salvation at work.

My prayer is for you.

Father! I am asking You to saturate every page of this book with Your healing power!

As You, Lord, performed many miracles with the hands of Apostle Paul (Acts 19:11), so let my hands (which are now being used to write the truth about healing) serve You, so that You could raise these people up, teach them not to look at the visible and to dare do the impossible. Lord, let these pages of the healing message be the point of contact with Your Spirit, like the handkerchiefs and aprons form Paul's body were, when illnesses ceased and demons went out (Acts 19:12).

I am attaching my heart to this prayer. My great desire is that everyone who ever reads this book will never stop nourishing their faith, neither get cold nor move away from You, Lord, so that no trickery or deception of this dead world could steal them from Your healing hand.

I thank You, Father!

Recommended Literature

1. New King James Version (NKJV Bible)
2. Kenneth E. Hagen "The Basics of spiritual growth", 1991
3. John G. Lake "Power over demons, diseases and death", 2008
4. Katherine Kulman "I believe in miracles"
5. Makhesh Chavda "The hidden power of a believer's touch", 2003
6. Smith Wigglesworth "Endlessly growing faith", 2007
7. John G. Lake "The diary of a God's general", 2007
8. Kenneth and Gloria Copeland "Pursuit of His Presence", 2009
9. Oral Roberts "Keeping on doing impossible things"
10. PDave Roberson "Power born of the Spirit"("The Walk of the Spirit – the walk of Power"), 2008
11. Kenneth E. Hagin "The Believer's Authority", 2007
12. Makhesh Chavda "The hidden power of prayer and fast", 2007
13. Gloria Copeland "Fellowship with the faithful" (from the magazine "Believer's Voice of Victory", 2008).
14. Kenneth E. Hagen "The Holy Spirit and His gifts", 2007

what I did to battle the disease
(A Guide for overcoming an illness)

I was constantly listening to the radio programmes and sermons about healing and faith. As long as you listen, your faith grows. As long as your faith grows, your ability to resist illness grows.

I was reading the Word of God (the Bible) and believed that it was "health to a man's whole body" (Proverbs 4:22). The word is like water in the spiritual world. It penetrates like mixture and influence on our physical body. "The word accomplishes what God desires and achieves the purpose for which He sent it" (Isaiah 55:11).

I searched for the Scripture verses about healing, bookmarked the pages with those verses and read them over and over (I was taking that "medicine" by my eyes and ears not by mouth). As a result I began to think the way it was written in the Bible.

I not only knew and read, but also spoke out loud about the fact that God heals, putting into practice the words "by His wounds I have been healed" (1Peter 2:24). I repeated them many times. This confession began to change my situation.

I realized that a man cannot heal another man. A human being does not have an ability to heal. He can only perform a physical action; a treatment. The root of all diseases is sin, and it lies in a spiritual world, in another dimension. Spiritual problems is something we should solve spiritually. We cannot reach the spiritual world with medications and physical therapy.

I contemplated on the fact that healing was not "something" but "Someone"- Jesus, the Word of God (Mark 4:38-41 "Where is your faith?"). We need to keep our focus on Jesus, because the healing is in Him.

I also realized that my hope had no other ground for support except for Jesus. I had to dare to believe God, Whom I did not see, more than the symptoms that I saw and felt. I kept on saying: "I do not live by what I see and feel but by the Word of God".

I did not call the visible things as they were (however paradoxically it sounds), but instead I constantly confessed the Word. Such a confession can gradually change the real situation, when you do not call things by their real names, but say what the Word says. Visible things become temporary if you do not speak according to what you feel, but according to what is written in the Bible.

I was doing that constantly, even when my physical condition worsened. Such a worsening can be the answer to our prayer for healing (there is no comfort for demons if they have to share a body with the spirit that is confirmed in God's truth).

I was looking for the believers who had walked the same path I was and emerged victorious. I talked to them, proclaimed the victory to come. The one who is winning the battle always has the power: he prays and speaks with daring and authority.

I stayed away from those people who felt pity for me, who inevitably sowed the words of doubt, disbelief and depression...People who have a diagnosis like mine, but are full of doubt and put their trust in men alone, they are setting themselves up to die.

I came to understand that disease is a consequence of sin. 2000 years ago Jesus nailed sin to the Cross on Calvary. That is why there is no sin in you. Jesus redeemed you from sin (soul) and disease (flesh): two parts of one. Healing is an integral part of salvation. What do we heal?

I was exercising in fast and prayer ("Nothing will be impossible for you", "However, this kind does not go out except by prayer and fasting").

I waited for my healing. Healing might not happen immediately or even within 24 hours. It is a process that starts from the inside. Our mind becomes renewed. The healing gets rooted in our mind, then becomes flesh and blood, and is then displayed in the body.

I found people who sought healing like I did and I told them about Jesus (another good way to confess healing into your life).

I forgave everyone I possibly could, gave back everything that did not belong to me, repented of my sins.

I was testifying, listening, reading. And believing. Why do I keep re-reading Katherine Kulman's book? For myself! I am constantly warming up my belief in the divine healing. Like the law have you are now under. What law? The law of Spirit of Life (Romans 8:2).

I realized that the vicinity of the hospital is not the best place for healing. In a hospital atmosphere Satan's diagnosis is constantly reinforced in spite of being destroyed. What can destroy it? Chemical medicines? No! The Word can!

P.S.The symptoms can come return. What should we do then? The same!

There following are the organizations that the home group of Irina Belova-Smorzh (www.raku-NET.ucoz.ru), provides mentorship and assistance to:

- Onco-hematology unit of Kiev region hospital (Baggoutovskaya Str., 1-9);
- Kiev hospice of the hospital #10 in Kiev (Goloseevskij Prospectus, 59);
- Kiev Municipal Children's Shelter #1 (Mayakovskij Prospectus, 28-B);
- Kiev Special Needs Boarding school #17 for children with mental and physical development problems (Ushinskogo Str, 15).

If you are interested in purchasing the book
wholesale please contact us at:
Tel.:+38 067 4081459
e-mail: thewayua@gmail.com

If you are interested in participating in these charities, or you would like to give a donation for the distribution of this book in treatment facilities where people cannot afford to buy it themselves, please contact us:
Tel.: +38 067 4081459
e-mail: thewayua@gmail.com

Irina Belova-Smorzh

BEING HEALED
AND STAYING ALIVE

19317684R00081

Printed in Great Britain
by Amazon